# The Way Ahead

# The Way Ahead

Church of England schools
in the new millennium

GS 1406

Church House Publishing
Church House,
Great Smith Street,
London SW1P 3NZ

ISBN 978-0-7151-4340-7

Published 2001 for the Church Schools Review Group by Church House Publishing

Copyright © The Archbishops' Council 2001

Typeset in Sabon 10.5

Cover design by Visible Edge

Printed in Great Britain by
Creative Print and Design Group,
Ebbw Vale, Wales

All rights reserved. No part of this publication may be reproduced or stored or transmitted by any means or in any form, electronic or mechanical, including photocopying, recording, or any information storage and retrieval system, without written permission which should be sought from the Copyright and Contracts Administrator, The Archbishops' Council, Church House, Great Smith Street, London SW1P 3NZ. (Tel: 020 7898 1557; Fax: 020 7898 1449; Email: copyright@c-of-e.org.uk).

This report has only the authority of the Group that produced it.

# Contents

| | |
|---|---|
| Membership of the Church Schools Review Group | vii |
| *Preface* | ix |
| Executive summary | xi |
| *chapter 1* Introduction | 1 |
| *chapter 2* Some history | 6 |
| *chapter 3* Why Church schools: for what purpose and for whom? | 9 |
| *chapter 4* Distinctiveness and partnership | 19 |
| *chapter 5* Proposals for increased provision | 34 |
| *chapter 6* Teachers, teachers, teachers | 45 |
| *chapter 7* The ministry, the Church and the parish | 53 |
| *chapter 8* Leadership, management and governance | 60 |
| *chapter 9* The Church colleges | 65 |
| *chapter 10* Summary of recommendations | 75 |
| *appendix 1* Differences between categories of Church schools | 83 |
| *appendix 2* Church schools by diocese | 85 |
| *appendix 3* Church of England secondary school GCSE results and other statistics | 87 |
| *appendix 4* Anglican colleges in England and Wales | 89 |
| *appendix 5* Vocation by the Archbishop of Wales | 91 |
| *appendix 6* Membership of subgroups | 93 |
| *appendix 7* Glossary of abbreviations and other terms | 96 |

# Membership of the Church Schools Review Group

**Chairman**  Lord Dearing CB

**Members**  Mrs Linda Borthwick
*Director of Education, Southwark Diocesan Board of Education*

Mr Peter Crook
*Director of The Lichfield Foundation and Deputy Director of the Midlands Leadership Centre*

The Revd Peter Hill
*Vicar of Calverton, Diocese of Southwell*

Dr John Rea
*Principal of the College of St Mark and St John, Plymouth*

Ms Christine Whatford
*Director of Education, London Borough of Hammersmith and Fulham*

Mrs Julie Wilks
*Head of Archbishop Runcie CE VA First School, Gosforth, Newcastle-upon-Tyne*

The Most Revd Dr Rowan Williams
*Archbishop of Wales*

**Assessors**  The Most Revd Vincent Nichols
*RC Archbishop of Birmingham*

Professor Arthur Pollard
*Emeritus Professor of English, Hull University; Member of the Church of England Board of Education 1991–2000 and Chairman of the Schools Committee to May 2001*

Mrs Oona Stannard
*Director, Catholic Education Service*

**Secretary**  Mr Colin Hopkins

**Adviser**  The Revd Canon John Hall
*General Secretary of the Church of England Board of Education and the National Society*

# Preface

## To the Archbishops' Council

1. We offer this final report in response to the remit you gave us to advise on the achievements and future development of Church of England schools. Much of our work builds on the excellent work of the dioceses and the Church of England Board of Education and National Society over the past fifteen years.

2. For all of us it has been a real privilege to be invited to advise at a time when society is increasingly welcoming to the contribution of the churches to education, and when the Church, through the General Synod, has identified the Church of England's schools as being at the centre of the Church's mission to the nation. We are conscious that much of what we have to say is a challenge, but a positive challenge, to the whole Church community at every level. We have consciously aimed very high, whilst recognizing that our future achievement, particularly in increasing secondary provision, by no means lies within the gift of the Church alone. But there is much, especially in terms of the way we think as a Church and the action we take, that does lie in our hands, and in these things lies the heart of our message.

3. Our warmest thanks go to all those who have contributed to our work: to the diocesan boards of education; to those listed in Appendix 6 who contributed to the work of our subgroups; and to the many individuals and organizations who have submitted evidence or responded to our consultation. A list of all those who have helped us in our task can be viewed on the National Society website (www.natsoc.org.uk). Our thanks go also to the many Church schools and colleges we have visited for making us so welcome.

4. We offer our grateful thanks to our three assessors, the Most Revd Vincent Nichols, Professor Arthur Pollard and Mrs Oona Stannard, and to our Adviser, the Revd Canon John Hall. We also thank his colleagues in the Church of England Board of Education and National Society, especially Mr Alan Brown, Mrs Liz Carter, Ms Daphne Griffith and Mr David Lankshear. They have all given generously of their time and wisdom. We warmly thank the Allchurches Trust Ltd, the Central Church Fund and the National Society for their generous grants towards the cost of the Review Group. Our thanks go also to Mr Mark Warbrooke, who helped in the research, to Mrs Pauline Ford who typed the drafts of this report, and to Mr Henry Head who helped in the analysis of consultation responses.

5. Our greatest debt is to our Secretary, Mr Colin Hopkins, whose commitment to the task has been well beyond the call of duty. The flow of paper has been immense and the resources available to him very small, and yet,

thanks to him, all proceedings have been well ordered, well recorded, and now finally reported.

*Signed*

Ron Dearing (Chairman)
Linda Borthwick
✠ Rowan Cambrensis
Peter Crook
Peter Hill
John Rea
Christine Whatford
Julie Wilks

17 April 2001

# Executive summary

1. The General Synod and the Archbishops' Council have identified Church schools as standing at the centre of the Church's mission to the nation. Our work over the last eighteen months has confirmed the crucial importance of Church schools to the whole mission of the Church to children and young people, and indeed to the long-term well-being of the Church of England.

2. The Church's mission can only be discharged through Church schools if there is a sufficiency of these schools across the land. We found very large variations in provision between one diocese and another, and in particular – in contrast to the Roman Catholic Church – small provision of secondary schools in relation to primary places. This leads to a growing imbalance between the ability of many Church secondary schools to offer places and the parental demand for them. A recent survey of some eighty Church of England secondary schools showed that for every 100 places there were 160 applications. We therefore recommend that over the next seven to eight years the Church seeks, in partnership with local authorities, to provide – whether through additional Church secondary schools or the expansion of existing schools – the equivalent of an extra 100 Church secondary schools (see Chapter 5).

3. We note that primary school provision is also varied, and recommend that dioceses should strengthen their provision where it is particularly sparse (Chapter 5).

4. To facilitate the proposed expansion, we recommend national fundraising to assist dioceses, and that the objective should be to raise £25 million over seven years (Chapter 5).

5. Expansion of provision is not enough. To be at the heart of the Church's mission, Church schools must be distinctively Christian and we make recommendations to secure best practice (Chapter 4).

6. Nor can Church schools be fully engaged in the Church's mission at parish level unless they are in close partnership with the worshipping community, and we make a range of practical recommendations to develop this partnership (Chapter 7).

7. We welcome action by recent Governments to bring the Church into partnership in the provision of schools and thereby widen parental choice. Central to our thinking is the growing partnership between diocesan and local education authorities, and we make recommendations on the way this partnership can develop (Chapter 4).

8. No factor will be more important in determining the future of Church schools than the Church's ability to recruit Christian teachers and develop heads and deputy heads to provide the excellent leadership that will be

needed in the additional secondary schools we propose. This will be crucial if, as we recommend, the Church should be especially concerned to serve areas of great economic and social need. We make recommendations accordingly, and on encouraging the vocation to teach (Chapter 6).

9. We support an ecumenical approach to new schools, and make recommendations for strengthening the links between maintained Church schools and independent schools that have an Anglican foundation, which we see as an important part of the family of Church schools (Chapter 5).

10. We make recommendations for the training of clergy, primarily at the post-ordination stage, to equip them to be both effective and welcome in schools (Chapter 7).

11. In our final chapter, we turn to the Church colleges of higher education where we make recommendations to secure and enhance their Christian distinctiveness, and to secure their long-term future (Chapter 9).

12. As a general theme throughout our report, we urge all elements in the Church community to look afresh at the way they work together, for in a community of purpose the work of the Church will be enhanced. We have in mind in particular the relationship between the parish and the Church school; the working relationships between the Church colleges, one with another, and their relationships with dioceses and schools.

13. In conclusion, we have a clear view that this is a time of opportunity for the Church, when there is much goodwill towards Church schools both at the national level from main political parties and at the local level, from many parents, and encouragement to increase the provision of Church schools. Our report is offered as a contribution to developing a way ahead. We make a full statement of our recommendations at the end of our report (Chapter 10).

*chapter 1*
# Introduction

**1.1** We were appointed by the Archbishops' Council, 'to review the achievements of Church of England schools and to make proposals for their future development'. In detail, our terms of reference continue:

> '1. Believing that Church schools stand at the centre of the Church's mission to the nation: to identify what currently contributes to the success and effectiveness of Church schools; and to examine the case for strengthening their distinctiveness and the means by which this might be achieved. (Effectiveness)
>
> 2. To undertake a clear assessment of the need and opportunities to increase the number of all Church schools, but in particular at the secondary phase, and how this might be achieved. (Strategic Development)
>
> 3. To develop strategies for increasing vocations to teach; and to review the particular and distinctive role of the Church colleges in the professional formation of Christian teachers and headteachers (both within Church schools and within the education system generally). (Vocation)
>
> 4. To make recommendations concerning these three areas.'

**1.2** We published an interim progress report in July 2000 and a Consultation Report in mid-December of that year in which we invited comment on our provisional recommendations and sought help in developing our thinking on several issues.

**1.3** The scale of the response to consultation was almost overwhelming but encouraging. Not everyone, notably the British Humanist Association and the National Secular Society, agreed with us. Neither of these organizations accepts education in schools which have a basis in one of the faiths. Some others challenged particular aspects of our thinking. But the weight of comment was supportive, and in general the local authorities which responded welcomed the emphasis we placed on a partnership with them. We have noted from public comment and the content of the government Green Paper of February 2001, Schools Building on Success (CM 5050), that central government has welcomed a relationship of partnership as much as local government. We believe Church schools have the goodwill of the other two main national political parties.

**1.4** In offering this final report we have therefore used the Consultation Report as our text, amending and extending it to reflect the comments and contributions we have found persuasive. We have been concerned, however, not to lose the thrust of the Consultation text by introducing all the detail that came from consultations. We see our report as a 'Pathfinder' which outlines a clear way ahead for consideration by the Archbishops' Council. Where it is needed, we see practical guidance on implementation being filled out by small expert working groups, whether at national or diocesan level. We would, however, urge that any such groups work to a tight timetable of no more than a few months so that the impetus for action, which we hope this report will provide, is not lost in a weight of detail and a burden of paper.

**1.5** Everything we have to say has its roots in, and derives its validity from, the Resolution of the General Synod in 1998 captured in our terms of reference in the words:

> *Believing that Church schools stand at the centre of the Church's mission to the nation.*

This Resolution challenges everyone in the Church to consider the implications of this statement of the importance and the place of Church schools, alongside the parish churches, at the heart of the Church's mission to the nation. We have sought in this report to spell out what this means.

**1.6** In particular it means that:

- all Church schools must be distinctively and recognizably Christian institutions;
- we must address in particular the lack of secondary provision in many areas, so that the mission can in fact be discharged throughout the nation;
- at all levels in the Church, in the schools, the parishes, the deaneries and within dioceses as well as in the Church colleges and theological colleges, courses and schemes, we need to consider afresh how, by working more closely together in true partnership, each can contribute more fully to the lives and well-being of the others, so that together we may all realize the opportunities before us.

**1.7** Perhaps the most challenging achievement of these is the third. It requires a change to established patterns of thinking and doing. It is a challenge that can all too easily be lost in the press of daily events, not least because it may mean giving a lower priority to some activities which are valued and reflect well established practice.

**1.8** To illustrate our wish for close integration, instead of a relationship at the level of the parish which might be diagramatically expressed thus

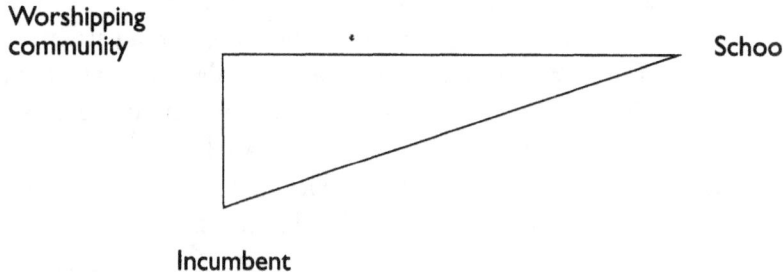

it should be like this, with the school at the heart of parish life:

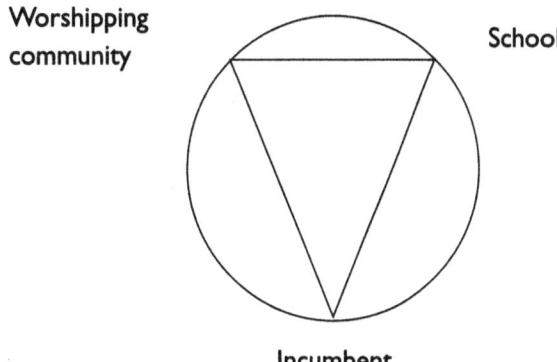

The school and Church are close together in partnership: the school and parish church see themselves as in active association – as an extended community – together at the heart of the Church's mission to the community.

**1.9** The closer coming together in active partnership of all parts of the extended Church community is a continuing theme of this report. We invite all members of the Church family of institutions to recognize the added strength that can be given and gained from strengthening the bonds between them and from breaking through any compartmental thinking.

**1.10** There will be those who, having read what we see as the implications of putting the Church school at the centre of the Church's mission, will question the validity of the Resolution of the General Synod. We recognize that some parts of our report may be considered radical. As we said in the first paragraph of the Introduction to our Consultation Report, we believe the General Synod judged well in passing its Resolution because the Church schools reach out to the young in far greater numbers than regularly attend church, and because through the young the Church is reaching out to parents and communities who would not otherwise engage with it. We develop our reasons for this conclusion in Chapter 3.

**1.11** However, no Church school can be considered as part of the Church's mission unless it is distinctively Christian.

**1.12** To put that assertion in a historical context, the Church created schools in huge numbers in the nineteenth century to offer basic education to the poor at a time when the state did not. It did so to enable human beings made in the image of God to realize their potential and to escape from poverty and degradation. Today, the state is a willing provider, and the purpose of the Church in education is not simply to provide the basic education needed for human dignity. That purpose is to offer a spiritual dimension to the lives of young people, within the traditions of the Church of England, in an increasingly secular world.

**1.13** The Church today still wishes to offer education for its own sake as a reflection of God's love for humanity. But the justification for retaining and aspiring to extend its provision, as recommended in this report, cannot be simply this, when the state is willing to provide as never before and when there are so many calls on the Church's limited resources. It is, and must be, because that engagement with children and young people in schools will, in the words of the late Lord Runcie when he was Archbishop of Canterbury, enable the Church to:

> Nourish those of the faith;
> Encourage those of other faiths;
> Challenge those who have no faith.

**1.14** That nourishment, that encouragement and that challenge can only be offered to the extent that the Church has schools that are sufficient in number, sufficiently distinctive in their spiritual life, and staffed by sufficient numbers of Christian teachers, to enable the Church to discharge its mission through schools. Each represents a challenge to the Church. Consideration of these three central issues leads us into many other areas relevant to providing those sufficiencies, most notably amongst them, the integration of Church schools into the life of parish churches and the future and character of the Church colleges of higher education, upon both of which the realization of the aspirations for the Church, which we offer in this report, depend in large measure. These three issues are at the heart of everything else that we have to say.

**1.15** On each of our chosen three issues there is much to be done. The opportunity for the Church is correspondingly great. The present provision of schools is the product of the great achievements of an earlier age. The challenge now is to build on those achievements so that the Church schools reach out to communities created in the last 50 years, and much more extensively to the secondary phase of education, which was not part of the work of the Church missionaries for education in the nineteenth century. The Church must reaffirm and develop its mission to the education of those who have least in life, whether in the towns or in rural communities. This was the inspiration behind the Church's massive expansion in education 200 years ago. And, most fundamental of all, the Church must foster the vocation to teach among Christians. To that end, it must show its commitment to Christian teachers in Community as well as Church schools. It must support them in their task at the level of the parish and the diocese. It must continue to be active at national level in influencing the development of Government policy in a way that recognizes the personal and professional needs of teachers. It must be immediately concerned to develop Christian teachers who have the potential and the desire to become head teachers and deputy heads in its schools. In all this, the Church must work in partnership and agreement with others, and especially through local education authorities.

**1.16** We recognize that action on some of our proposals cannot be achieved by the Church alone. This is especially so of our proposals for creating the equivalent of 100 more Church secondary schools, the achievement of which, even if the necessary funding can be secured, is dependent on the support of others. The response to our consultation has underlined that even where there may be goodwill in principle to establishing additional Church schools, circumstances will be powerful in determining the timetable, and also that the achievement of 100 schools in say five years is well beyond what dioceses thought could be achieved. We respect such counsel and respond to it in Chapter 5. But we think it right that the whole Church, in responding to the Resolution of the General Synod, should accept the challenge to ensure that our primary and secondary schools can in fact be at the heart of the Church's mission to all parts of the nation.

**1.17** The present is a time when parents and policy makers are showing their regard for what the Church schools have to offer to children of all faiths and none. Perhaps as never before in 50 years, the Church has a great opportunity to pursue and develop its mission to the nation through its schools. We therefore encourage the Church to see this report as offering a response to this opportunity: as outlining a desired 'Way Ahead'.

*chapter 2*
# Some history

**2.1** The Church's commitment to the provision of education extends over many centuries. It was most powerfully evident in its drive for the mass provision of Christian education for the poor in the early and middle years of the nineteenth century. Its principal instrument was the National Society, created in 1811. By the time of the national census of 1851, forty years later, the Church had established 17,000 schools.

**2.2** State provision for public education did not come until the Education Act of 1870, and it operated by supplementing rather than replacing voluntary provision. This Act was a significant moment in the development of the practice of partnership between the state and the churches in education, and one from which we believe society has greatly benefited.

**2.3** This report is not the occasion for tracing the history of the provision for education since the 1870 Act. A snapshot of provision shortly after the turn of that century would show that the voluntary sector then numbered over 14,000 schools of which rather more than 1,000 were Roman Catholic, with a further similar number provided by the Wesleyans and others. At the time of the outbreak of the Second World War, after seventy years of state provision, the voluntary sector, i.e. the churches, were together still providing schooling for nearly a third of the children of school age.

**2.4** However, the Church had lacked the capital to match the quality of premises and equipment of State schools, and the quality of education was suffering. The Education Act of 1944 provided a new deal in which Church schools were offered the option of increased State funding and control as 'Voluntary Controlled schools' or lesser State support and greater independence as 'Voluntary Aided schools'. At the same time, the 1944 Act required all schools to have a daily act of collective worship and religious instruction. The 1944 Act extended the school leaving age to fifteen and provided for secondary education in separate schools between the ages of eleven and fifteen.

**2.5** The 1944 Act was thus a significant turning point in the history of Church schools. In the light of the provisions of that Act, it is thought that the Government expected most Church schools to choose to become 'Voluntary Controlled'. In fact, the Methodist Church continued a pre-existing policy of reducing the number of its schools, and the number of maintained Methodist schools has declined from its nineteenth-century maximum of 900 to some 57 today, half of them in partnership with the Church of England. Neither the Anglican nor the Roman Catholic Churches adopted that policy: indeed in the 1950s and 1960s the Roman Catholic Church expanded its school provision vigorously, especially at the secondary level. By comparison, the expansion in Anglican secondary schools was modest and the number of its primary schools declined.

**2.6** The number of pupils in Anglican and Roman Catholic schools has developed as follows since 1950:

|  | PRIMARY | | SECONDARY | |
|---|---|---|---|---|
|  | Anglican | RC | Anglican | RC |
| 1950 | 844 | 329 | 64 | 50 |
| 2000 | 774 | 411 | 150 | 309 |
|  | *(thousands)* | | | |

Source: DfEE

**2.7** Within the overall number, in 2000 rather more than half of the Church of England schools were in the Voluntary Controlled category. By contrast the Roman Catholic Church pursued a policy of Voluntary Aided status.

**2.8** Over the post-war years there have been progressive developments in legislative provision, and the implications of a school being in the Voluntary Aided and Controlled categories have changed. (We summarize what each category means at the present time in Appendix 1.) There is a third category of Foundation schools, which often were Grant Maintained schools, but the number of Foundation Church of England schools today is small.

**2.9** Perhaps the most significant of these Acts, in terms of the recommendations in this report, was the School Standards and Framework Act 1998, which amongst other things provides for the following:

- The creation of School Organization Committees comprising representatives of the local education authority, the Anglican and Roman Catholic Churches, governing bodies and the Learning and Skills Council to decide on proposals to establish, close, alter or change the category of a school. (Powers previously exercised by the Secretary of State were delegated to these local committees; in the absence of agreement a decision is taken by a statutory adjudicator appointed by the Secretary of State.)

- The creation of widely based Admission Forums to consider admissions to schools.

- A governing body, in considering candidates for appointment to the post of headteacher in Voluntary Controlled or Foundation Schools, to 'have regard to the candidate's ability and fitness to preserve and develop the religious character of the school'. In Voluntary Aided schools the governing body may decide in appointing headteachers and other teachers to give explicit preference to committed members of the Church of England or other Christian churches.

- A governing body can choose to change from the Voluntary Controlled to the Voluntary Aided category without initial financial penalty.

**2.10** The effect of these changes is to bring the churches more substantially into the decision-taking mechanism at local level and to make these decisions a matter for collective agreement rather than for any one party. At both national and local levels the Church works in a partnership with government. It is a partnership that the Church very much welcomes, and wishes to develop as fundamental to its whole approach to education.

**2.11** The Green Paper proposals (CM 5050) of February 2001 are material to the recommendations in this report for increasing the Church's secondary provision. They reduce the Governors' capital contribution to Voluntary Aided schools from 15 to 10 per cent and outline an approach in which faith sponsors and others may take responsibility for some schools on fixed term renewable contracts. We refer to these proposals in later chapters.

*chapter 3*
# Why Church schools: for what purpose and for whom?

> Reflecting on his former experience as the Chairman of a diocesan board of education, one retired bishop wrote to us saying:
>
> 'I came to the job thinking Church schools were an ecclesiastical irrelevance: I left it convinced that they are jewels in the ecclesiastical crown'

**3.1** The statement in our terms of reference that the Church schools stand at the centre of the Church's mission to the nation has the authority of the General Synod and the Archbishops' Council. Action on this report must however be based on conviction as well as authority. We are moreover aware that what may be desirable in the light of Synod's Resolution has not been the practice in all parishes.

> One diocese in its consultation response said:
>
> 'We feel that there is much ground to be covered, many hearts and minds to be engaged and won over before the nub of the motion (i.e. the General Synod motion) is in place in the mind of the Church. This is particularly true when it comes to matters relating to schools' relationships with clergy and their relationships with parishes, deaneries and dioceses.'

**3.2** We are also conscious that what we have to say in Chapter 7 requires a reassessment both of the training of clergy and of the way some parish churches respond to Church schools and Christian teachers in Community schools. We therefore begin with our own reflections on the desirability of Church schools being in fact at the centre of the Church's mission.

## The Church's need to reach the young

**3.3** The Church has a major problem in attracting young people to its services as a means of discharging its mission, and one that causes much concern. This bears directly on the future of the Church.

**3.4** In contrast the Church has some 900,000 young people attending its schools. Not all of these schools are everything that they might be, but our experience is that the vast majority give their pupils the experience of the meaning of faith and of what it is to work and play in a community that seeks to live its beliefs and values. We set out in section 4.6 what we see as the fundamental characteristics of a Church school. These include meaningful daily worship and quality religious education as well as a distinctively Christian ethos.

**3.5** We do not have a detailed analysis of Church attendance by young people under and over eleven years old. Observation suggests that attendance by those over eleven is a modest proportion of the 175,000 children who are currently counted as attending Church services on Sunday. One of the Review Group's central concerns is that, with our limited provision for this age group in Church secondary schools, we are not able to provide secondary school places for more than one in five of the children attending Church primary schools. This means that we are losing contact with most of the Church primary school children just at the time of life when they need answers to their questions and support in their faith. It is not that there is a lack of demand for places in many of our secondary schools. We comment elsewhere on their popularity (see 5.9) The gap between available places and demand for them is increasing: a reverse image of attendance at church services.

**3.6** We conclude that while current practice in some parishes, and perhaps many, may not place Church schools at the centre of their mission, without the Church schools the Church would be reaching only a small minority of young people. We also conclude that the Christian life of parishes and the experience of staff and pupils in Church schools are enriched once there is an affirming relationship between them, and we have more to say on this in Chapter 7. The closer the schools are to the centre of the mission of the parish, the better for parish and school.

**3.7** From observation we would add that, while we have had reports that in a small number of cases Church schools have lost their distinctiveness, this is far from the case in the many schools we have visited. These visits have often been heart-warming experiences, with the school's Christian character being evident as a continuing statement to the surrounding community of the Church as a living reality, seeking to practise what it preaches in a way that is wholly meaningful in a busy world.

**3.8** We have also noted that through the children attending its schools, the Church has an opportunity to reach out to parents. The 900,000 children provide access to parents, very many of whom would otherwise have no contact with the Church.

> The Diocese of London said in its evidence:
>
> The Archbishop of York, as Bishop of London, was fond of pointing out that clergy will meet far more family members in a school than they are likely to encounter in Sunday services.

As of necessity adults will increasingly be engaged in the practice of lifelong learning. If Church schools can become family learning centres in response to this development, so also the opportunity to reach out to parents will be enhanced.

**3.9** It has been put to us that a measure of the effectiveness of Church schools should be found in the number of young people they bring into Church services or other Church activities for children. Whether they come into Church or not, Church schools are giving them the opportunity to know Christ, to learn in a community that seeks to live by his word, and to engage in worship. Where pupils come from homes which are not Christian, or only nominally Christian with parents who have little knowledge of the Bible, this is a gift they would not otherwise experience. For those from Christian homes it will help to develop their faith and endow them with knowledge they can pass on to their own children. To the extent that they do not go to church in their teen years or in their twenties, it may well be that the Christian grounding at school will bring them into church when they have families of their own. The justification for Church schools lies in offering children and young people an opportunity to experience the meaning of the Christian faith.

## What do we mean by Church schools being *at* the centre of the mission of the Church to the nation?

**3.10** We do not take the Resolution of the General Synod to mean that Church schools **are the centre** of the Church's mission, but as the Resolution says, 'at the centre'. We take this to mean that they stand alongside the parish churches, which lead the missionary work of the Church, as an integral part of the Church community, offering Christ to the young and through them, to varying degrees, offering parents the opportunity to learn from children and to engage in the life of a Christian institution. As one headteacher aptly put it of her school at one of our consultation meetings, 'We do not admit children, we admit families.' In its full realization, then, a Church school admits families to its community with the child, and in so doing enriches family life. Through partnership with families the Church is better able to foster the educational achievement of pupils. **It should be a special objective of every Church school to engage the parents in the education and the broader school life of the child.** In this way the school enlarges its mission of service and of nurture.

## The Church's mission to the nation

**3.11** If the Church schools are at the centre of the Church's mission, their work must derive from the mission of the whole Church. In a sentence, the Church's mission is to open up people to what God desires for them: Church schools are places where a particular vision of humanity is offered. More fully, but still very briefly the mission of the Church is:

> to proclaim the gospel;
>
> to nourish Christians in their faith;
>
> to bring others into the faith;
>
> and
>
> to nurture and maintain the dignity of the image of God in human beings through service, speaking out on important issues and to work for social justice as part of that mission.

## Our purposes in Church schools

**3.12** These elements are present in the proposals we offer for consideration in this report. Church schools are places where the faith is lived, and which therefore offer opportunities to pupils and their families to explore the truths of Christian faith, to develop spiritually and morally, and to have a basis for *choice* about Christian commitment. They are places where the beliefs and practices of other faiths will be respected. Church schools are not, and should not be, agents of proselytism where pupils are *expected* to make a Christian commitment.

**3.13** Turning now to the distinctive mission of the Church schools within the Church, we see it as an important and challenging part of our task to offer advice on that mission for the present times. In doing so, we would counsel that today's Church should be respectful of what was achieved by previous generations in responding to the needs of their times as they saw them, and of the devoted way in which a host of Christians today is carrying their work onward. Our concern is to support them in their ongoing tasks, in very varying and changing circumstances; to offer a developmental way forward, which will need to be interpreted according to the circumstances in which individual schools find themselves; and in particular to offer some guidelines to the dioceses in giving effect to our recommendations on expanding provision.

**3.14** Our statement of the purpose of the Church in its Church schools is one that reflects the needs and opportunities of the present times. When Matthew Arnold was writing his famous poem on the melancholy long withdrawing roar of the sea of faith along 'the vast edges drear / And naked shingles of the world'[1] in the nineteenth century, some two million children attended Sunday school. Today, the numbers are very different, **and if the children are not coming to us we must go to them. Church schools are the Church's major opportunity to serve young people. It is an opportunity more and more parents are asking the Church to take.**

**3.15** It would not have been possible for the Durham Commission of Enquiry[2] to write in these terms 30 years ago, when the Church's role in education was regarded with some scepticism, and the emphasis was being placed on the Church's mission of service to the community, through education, rather than on the role of the Church schools as combining a mission of service with that of nourishing children of the faith in their faith.

**3.16** The ministry of service is well established, and has historically been understood as the 'general' purpose of the Church in education as opposed to the 'domestic' purpose of offering education in a Christian context to the children of members of the Church of England. The general purpose proceeds from the fourth of the elements in the mission of the Church – work for human dignity – we identified in the eleventh paragraph of this chapter. It is underpinned by a theology of service. As put at a gathering of the World Council of Churches in 1968 (amended to include women as well as men):[3]

> 'It is a Christian's concern for the wholeness of the human being, for the quality of the common life, for the direction in which humanity goes, that turns us towards education now and sets us inside it and will not let us disengage.'

It expresses the Church's concern to serve all humanity as children of God.

**3.17** The hitherto expressed 'domestic' function proceeds from a theology of nurture: the nurture of the worshipping community, and the nurture of young people in and from the faith. From now on, we propose to use the terms 'service' and 'nurture' as our own description of the Church's purposes in education.

**3.18** Over the last 15 years in particular the priority the Durham Commission gave to the service function has come under increasing challenge. In a paper to the General Synod published in 1984 (*A Future in Partnership*) the case was made that in every Church school both the service and nurture purposes should be consciously present, the school contributing to the provision of general education in the neighbourhood whilst offering an education grounded in faith. The relationship between the Church and the state has developed into a willing partnership in which the distinctive contribution of the Church schools is welcomed. This spirit of partnership, which has characterized recent governments, has been reflected in a succession of legislative instruments over the last twelve years which have helped the Church to foster the Christian character of its schools and to engage at local level in partnership with other providers, and the local education authorities in particular.

## The balance between the service and nurture purposes of the Church in education

**3.19** The balance between the service and nurture purposes of the Church school is not one that can be prescribed for all time. It will rightly need to respond to the needs of the times. As we have said, since the time of the Durham Commission the nurture purpose of the Church, as part of a partnership with Community schools, has gained in emphasis. Following the increased standing of Church schools with parents and more generally with society, and the associated increase in demand for places, it has been inevitable that governing bodies in Voluntary Aided schools should respond to the demand from Christian parents. Moreover, in an increasingly secular society the Church is right to respond to the concern of Christian parents to give their children the opportunity to experience what it is to learn in a distinctively Christian environment.

**3.20** The only way in which the Church can adequately respond to that demand and continue to fulfil its service purpose is to expand the provision of places in Church schools. We recommended increased provision for secondary schools in our interim report in July 2000 and in our Consultation Report. We confirm such a recommendation now, and we also make recommendations for some increased provision in primary schools (see Chapter 5).

**3.21** In noting today's increased welcome for distinctive approaches to education, we see no dichotomy between the service and nurture purposes of the Church in education. Rather we see the Church serving the nation in a distinctive way as a gospel imperative. The Church has a commission to engage with society and its institutional structures precisely because there is good news to offer. It is part of the Church's wider sense of mission to society to engage with the community in a distinctive manner, recognizing the common elements within the experience of its people and sharing in their life. This compels us to be in education, and visibly in the bricks and mortar of our schools themselves.

**3.22** It was Christ's wish to 'let the little children come to me' (Mark 10:14). Today's society is one where medical and technological progress proceeds apace, often challenging once established norms of morality and ethical understanding. Telecommunications have seemingly made the whole world accessible at the touch of a button. Globalization and the ascendancy of consumerism have emphasized personal choice, but have not so far generated a balancing sense of community or a coherent sense of responsibility for sustaining the earth's own well-being or for the quality of our civilization. In a world of shifting sands, many parents have welcomed the stability offered by schools that offer an enduring alternative to the growingly secular values of society.

**3.23** In offering an invitation to children and young people from all backgrounds to participate in a Christian community, Church schools can provide a real experience of God's love for all humanity. In a Church school, pupils not only learn about religion but they can experience it as a living tradition and inheritance of faith. Church schools are therefore a unique gift from the Church to an increasingly secular culture. The Archbishop of Canterbury has written:[4]

> Church schools are as concerned as any other school to equip pupils for lives marked by rapid change, global competition and insecurity. But Church schools know in their viscera that this is not just about acquiring skills and good examination results. It is about forming people who have the moral strength and spiritual depth to hold to a course and weather ups and downs. It is about forming people who know that economic competition is not more important than family life and love of neighbour, and that technical innovation is not more important than reverence for the beauty of creation. It is about forming people who, however academically and technically skilful, are not reduced to inarticulate embarrassment by the great questions of life and death, meaning and truth. Church schools themselves embody the truth that a context of firm principles suffused by faith and love is the best and right basis for learning and growing.'

**3.24** We believe that the revelation of God's love for all humanity within a holistic approach to education is at the heart of the Church's purpose in our Church schools. This is reflected in the ethos statement that was offered to all Church schools two years ago after consultation with diocesan directors of education. It has been widely adopted, and reads:

> *Recognizing its historic foundation, the school will preserve and develop its religious character in accordance with the principles of the Church at parish and diocesan level.*
>
> *The school aims to serve its community by providing education of the highest quality within the context of Christian belief and practice. It encourages an understanding of the meaning and*

*significance of faith and promotes Christian values through the experience it offers all its pupils.*

**3.25** The way this ethos statement is interpreted will reflect the individual circumstances of schools, which vary greatly. But it will be the aspiration of all that Christian values and principles will, as one diocese put it in evidence to us, 'run through every area of school life as the writing runs through a stick of rock'. If the Church has a calling to participate in education, then it must be in a bold and decisive manner, not seeking to impose its faith but offering it as a gift to be experienced through the enjoyment pupils have in working in a community where Christian principles are practised.

**3.26** The gift is Christ. Through him the Church has a model of what it is to grow towards full humanity. The Church takes and derives its stand from the love of God and the commandment to love your neighbour. The Church has a clear point of reference that supports Christians in upholding the values of the faith. In this context, the Church school offers a spiritual and moral basis for the development of human wholeness and a sure foundation for personal and social values based on the person and ministry of Christ. The Church school offers a distinctive language for understanding life and interpreting human experience. As a community of faith, the Church school should, in its best expression, reflect the nature of the Trinity, a life shared and defined by reference to others. Here we can begin to discover who we are, why we are, and – perhaps most importantly – what we might be.

**3.27** Writing of 'the heart of education', the Archbishop of York has said:[5]

> 'The school is called to reflect these qualities: a fellowship and community which gives individuals scope fully to be themselves, yet participating equally in the common life. Furthermore, to stress that the school is a community of persons (reflecting the Trinitarian life) is to emphasize relationships; the personal is thus prior to the institutional; the institutional exists not for its own sake but solely for the purpose of nurturing and sustaining the relations of the persons who comprise any particular community or organization.'

**3.28** In a Church school, the offer of a Christian understanding of the world and the place of humanity in it will be reflected in worship. In particular, it will be reflected in the everyday life of the school, quietly respectful of the beliefs of others and of other faiths, but confident in its own faith. Church schools will not actively seek to convert children from the faith of their parents, but pupils will experience what it is to live in a community that celebrates the Christian faith; to work within a framework of discipline and yet to be confident of forgiveness; to begin to share the Christian's hope and the Christian experience that the greatest power in life and beyond it is selfless love.

## A policy of inclusiveness

**3.29** The Church's approach to education as a whole, while admitting of diversity of practice in the light of particular local circumstances, is one founded on a notion of inclusiveness rather than separation from the community.

The composition of its school population, especially in primary schools where parents generally want their children educated close to home, will reflect the composition of the neighbourhood and must therefore be inclusive of all ethnicity, belief and social class. The Church will seek to develop its provision as part of a wider partnership with communities. Its schools will seek to engage actively with all parents and to be distinctively welcoming to them.

**3.30** The policy of inclusiveness is most apparent in Church schools where, over the years, the community has become predominantly one of minority ethnic families, notably Muslim or Sikh. In these cases the school may be predominantly or even wholly of children of these faiths. We find that, in these cases, the schools are respectful of the faith of parents, but nevertheless offer the children an experience of the Christian faith, both through the everyday life of the school and through inclusive forms of worship. The advice to us was that parents welcome the opportunity to send their children to a faith school where there is belief in God.

**3.31** The policy of inclusiveness extends also to children of no faith where, without seeking to convert these children to the faith, the school offers the practice of faith, worship and a school life founded on Christian values, all of which give the children an opportunity to make an informed choice that they might otherwise not experience.

**3.32** The Diocese of London wrote movingly in its response to consultation in terms that could equally apply to some Community schools:

> In some [of our] schools, one only has to walk through the door and meet the children to know which part of the world is at war this week. In those schools, there are children who do not speak English, who have been traumatized by what they have witnessed, who have experienced real suffering and who can, within a few short weeks of being in a stable environment, begin to smile and play again. At school they can begin to flower again.

## Humanist and secular perspectives

**3.33** We are aware that during the course of our work opposition has been expressed to the concept of religious schools. In their evidence both the British Humanist Association (BHA) and the National Secular Society (NSS) have claimed that such schools are 'divisive' and exclusive and that they reduce parental choice. According to the National Secular Society, 'the more religious schools there are, the more divided society will become'. They see our proposals as 'a last ditch attempt [by the Church] to regain influence and support'. Both the BHA and NSS oppose the public funding of Church schools. It should be noted that primary legislation would be needed to abolish Church schools.

**3.34** Our view is that Church schools are a legitimate expression of diversity within the educational system. We question the assumption that religion is by its nature inescapably divisive, and the philosophical corollary of this assumption that only a 'secular' understanding of the world can be truly inclusive. We have noted on our visits that Church schools often have a widespread appeal to all sections of society, and that parents of other faiths often choose Church schools because they take faith seriously. Church schools are to be found in remote villages and in the heart of the inner cities. They represent the Church of England's visible commitment to the nation's education and service to many different types of community. Our position is that a Christian understanding of the world calls us to celebrate the individuality and equal value of all humanity. We therefore want to celebrate the diversity of our schools and the great range of children and young people they educate from all sections of society.

**3.35** A Christian understanding of life perceives God's creative, redemptive and transforming purpose in the whole of human activity. Church schools therefore have an important role in helping people – children and parents alike – to understand their part in working towards the common good as understood in a Christian society. In its educational role, the Church is working to serve that common good, and to develop greater mutual understanding, and is not aiming to promote a sectarian endeavour.

**3.36** This understanding leads us to conclude that the notions of distinctiveness and inclusiveness are not mutually exclusive. A distinctive approach to education needs to be matched by openness to all elements of society if introversion is to be avoided. That is the strength of the community of Church schools: Christ calls us to serve **all** people as an expression of our calling. We note that the British Humanist Association is 'in favour of integrated and inclusive schools, which can instil sound moral principles based on shared human experience'. Our own vision of inclusiveness is based on Christ's commandment to love all people, and his own sharing fully in the life of humanity: in his birth, in his own ministry of healing and teaching, and in his suffering, death and resurrection. Church schools are part of the body of Christ, and a visible recognition of the divine within human experience.

## Parental choice and educational standards

**3.37** Today the Church schools stand well in the regard of many parents of all faiths and no faith. The most powerful consideration with very many parents in choosing a school is its educational performance and that the distinctive needs of each child are understood. Many Church schools have earned a good reputation for these qualities. Even within Church schools that have not earned such a reputation, parents are often influenced by the security they feel from sending children to a school which they know has a well-grounded basis for its values and moral standards recognized even by those who are not practising Christians.

**3.38** In making this report on our findings, we are conscious that there are very many Community schools that have clear moral purposes and in which parents rightly have every confidence. We simply comment that we have found that the distinctive character of Church schools is attractive to many parents because it is inherent in their claim and practice to serve Christ.

**3.39** On educational performance, as we say above, many Church schools have earned a good reputation for educational results. Our recommendation for a substantial increase in Church secondary provision is not based on an argument that all do well in academic results. While visits brought home to us how excellent these schools can be, two of them in areas of great social disadvantage were in special measures, although we were glad to learn that one of them is now out of them. Church schools face the same difficulties as Community schools and in this report we stress the importance of the Church ensuring that in considering proposals for expanding its provision, it has the necessary high quality school leaders (see Chapter 5).

**3.40** Until recently there has been little analysis of the results of Church schools, and there is need for more. With the focus in our recommendations about provision of Church of England secondary schools, we have looked into their GCSE results. We find that the average point score is 12 per cent higher than in Community schools, a difference confirmed by independent research sent to us by Civitas. Another measure, the percentage getting A*–C passes, points in the same direction. Further information is given briefly in Appendix 3. The percentage receiving free school meals in Church secondary schools was 15 per cent as compared with 17 per cent in Community secondary schools.

**3.41** The concern of the Church, however, like that of parents is with individual children rather than with national averages and it must be the purpose of the Church to strive continually to achieve more for its pupils as individuals, in terms of results as conventionally assessed, and in their development as human beings. The Church should not be deterred from seeking especially to serve areas of social and economic deprivation by any adverse effect on the aggregate results of its schools.

**3.42** Our distinctive purpose and contribution in education is to offer Christ: to embrace the development of the spiritual life and awareness of young people. Our commitment is to developing the potential of each child as an individual, made in the image of God. This commitment means that we endorse the importance of raising standards of educational achievement in schools so that our children are equipped to live life fully and contribute to the lives of others. It also means that Church schools should react positively and decisively to any indication, following inspection, of scope for improvement or need to remedy any inadequate performance. The interests of the children require that in these circumstances action should be timely and effective.

**3.43** In so far as it lies within them, we want our children – every one of them – 'to do well', and the levels of school attainment, whether through teacher assessment, Standard Assessment Tests, the GCSE and so on, to be a source of real satisfaction to parents.

### Notes

1 *Dover Beach* (1867), lines 26–7.
2 *The Fourth R*, SPCK, 1970, was the Report of the Commission chaired by the then Bishop of Durham to enquire into Religious Education.
3 Quoted in *The Fourth R*.
4 'The Importance of Church schools', from *A Christian Voice in Education: Distinctiveness in Church Schools*, The National Society, 1988, pp. 9–10.
5 'A Christian Vision in Education', *A Christian Voice in Education*, pp. 13–14.

*chapter 4*
# Distinctiveness and partnership

**4.1** We have argued in Chapter 1 that with the state being a willing provider of education, the justification for the Church's presence in education must be to offer an approach to education that is distinctively Christian.

**4.2** There will be different interpretations of distinctiveness by governing bodies reflecting the role of the school in its community, its statutory category, the composition of the community, and the traditions of the local church. For example, if its statutory category is that of a Voluntary Controlled school its admissions policy will be determined by the local education authority in consultation with the governing body rather than by the governing body alone, and if it is the only school in a village its essential service will be to the local community. By contrast a Voluntary Aided secondary school in a city where there are many schools may be more concerned with serving the Christian community. There will be many variants of these two illustrations. A recent survey of Voluntary Aided schools showed that rather more than three quarters of them had a religious affiliation in their admissions criteria, but only a third of them had a religious category as the first criterion. In at least half of schools there was no need to put their oversubscription criteria into practice.

**4.3** Although for a range of reasons there will be variations between one Church school and another, there will be certain core principles and values that should unite all Church schools within the Christian mission. These will be the gospel values of loving God and one's neighbour, as well as the practical outworking of these values in how pupils are taught to conduct themselves and to relate to one another and to God's world.

**4.4** The distinctive identity of a Church school is enhanced by its relationship with a parish church (or churches where it serves a wide area), and for many secondary schools by access to a chaplaincy serving the school. We have found that the relationships with the incumbent of a parish church vary considerably. We comment in Chapter 7 on the role of the clergy and the relationship of Church schools to the parish generally, for it seems to us that the whole Church needs to develop a much clearer understanding of the role of Church schools within Christian ministry and their importance as centres of Christian community, where the Church offers service to all. In saying this, we acknowledge and welcome the strong links many parishes also have with Community and Foundation schools. It suffices to say here that a partnership between a Church school and a parish church has much to offer both the school and the parish within which it is situated. The relationship is at its best when the incumbent and other members of the church are a welcome and familiar presence, respecting and supporting the teachers, while the school seeks to involve itself in worship in the church from time to time, for example at the great festivals and at the end of the school year, and to welcome a new headteacher. Parishioners have an important duty to pray for their school on a regular basis, and indeed for all schools and the work of all teachers in them.

**4.5** The issue of distinctiveness is posed most directly for Voluntary Controlled schools serving an isolated village community where except on special occasions the practice of church attendance is for a small minority. Today's Church has inherited many hundreds of such primary schools from the nineteenth and twentieth centuries. **We recommend that these Voluntary Controlled primary schools serving village communities should remain primarily to serve those communities, but that in so doing they should always be and be seen to be distinctively Christian institutions.**

**4.6** We recommend for consideration that where they have not already done so governing bodies in all Church schools should adopt the ethos statement or one akin to it set out in paragraph 3.24 above and as a minimum:

- ensure that the school is led by a headteacher who is committed, with the help of staff, to establish and maintain the Christian character of the school in its day to day activities and in the curriculum;

- engage meaningfully in a real act of Christian worship every day;

- offer a school life that incorporates the values of the Christian faith as illustrated in paragraphs 3.28 and 4.8;

- ensure that religious education is given at least 5 per cent of school time and that the character and quality of religious education are a particular concern of the headteacher and the governing body;

- observe the major Christian festivals and in schools in which other faiths are present ensure that those faiths are able *and encouraged* to mark their major festivals with integrity;

- maintain and develop an active and affirming relationship with a parish church;

- proclaim that it is a Church of England school on its external signboard and on its stationery and make appropriate use of Christian symbols inside and outside the school.

**4.7** This is a minimum list, and we presume to offer it because we have found that from time to time and place to place the distinctiveness has been attenuated. In rare cases we find that the Church foundation of the school has been forgotten.

> One diocese commented in its evidence that on occasion it was approached by schools that were unsure why they were Church schools and reported that a further group would be difficult to distinguish from Community schools. Another diocese similarly recorded that some of its schools were hardly recognizable as Church schools, and asked for some strategic guidance on 'rechristianizing' them. A third said that 'at least one Church school has only been persuaded of its Church status in the last couple of years'.

We recognize that these cases are a small minority, and that Section 23 Inspections under the 1996 School Inspections Act (formerly introduced in Section 13 of the 1992 Education (Schools) Act) have brought the distinctiveness of Church schools into focus and challenged Church schools to reflect on and develop their distinctiveness as Christian institutions. Much has been achieved since 1992 to affirm the Christian foundation of Church schools. Nevertheless, these comments by dioceses point to the need to make clear – as above – the minimum practices of a Church school.

**4.8** Whilst there are certain fundamental values that typify Church schools, they should also provide a foundation of experience of the Christian life and a body of knowledge of the Christian faith that can sustain their pupils throughout their lives. This range of experience for a child able to attend a Church school through both primary and secondary schooling should include an explicit commitment to honesty and openness; a celebration of the identity and nature of culturally and ethnically diverse groups; a readiness to seek and offer forgiveness, all founded in a sense of the presence of God and of the numinous. It should include a knowledge of how to pray and of the liturgy, especially the Eucharist/Holy Communion; and an awareness of the challenge of the spiritual life within everyday experience.

**4.9** The experience of these things will be adapted to the child's own development. There should be respect for those of other faiths who cannot in conscience engage in the full liturgy of Christian worship. The Church school should strive to avoid a sense of exclusion by finding as much common ground between the faiths represented in the school as possible and by involving the leaders of other faiths as appropriate.

## The curriculum

**4.10** Church schools will follow the National Curriculum in the same way as Community schools. But the nationally prescribed curriculum allows scope for the individual school and the individual teacher to develop the knowledge, skills and understanding required by the curriculum through schemes of work that reflect the specialist knowledge of the teacher and the Christian character of the school. There will therefore be opportunities for teachers in Church schools to illustrate their teaching with examples that reflect the highest aspirations of humanity and to bring out the moral and ethical issues that face us. In doing so, teachers have occasion to show the relevance of the teaching of Christian and other faiths to the whole of human experience. They have an opportunity to demonstrate that educational 'effectiveness' is concerned with the development of the whole person as a child of God. It is part of the task of the national Church and the Church colleges of higher education to foster the development of programmes of work that will help Church schools to make that contribution to education.

**4.11** We warmly welcome the work of those engaged in developing methodologies for a distinctively Christian approach to the curriculum and materials for the theory and practice of Christian education. We also welcome the developmental work that has been taking place in a number of schools to give expression to their chosen ethos statements through class work and in so doing to engage in the spiritual, moral, social and cultural development of pupils required by Section 351 of the Education Act 1996. We are conscious that teachers need help in their initial training and in career development to bring this dimension of education meaningfully into everyday teaching of the curriculum.

## The importance of religious education

**4.12** An important element in the distinctiveness of Church schools will lie in the emphasis on the quality of religious education in the curriculum, which whilst covering other faiths will give particular weight to the Christian faith as held by the Church of England. The headteacher will see religious education and worship as a personal and professional care, and part of that care will be to ensure along with the (foundation) governors that the school has clear, coherent and professionally competent policies for both. The school will be concerned to offer teaching in religious education that is better than the satisfactory level required by inspectors. We note that Section 23 inspection has shown that virtually every Voluntary Aided primary and secondary school has a policy for religious education. Diocesan teams report generally that the quality of the teaching of RE and the quality of ethos and collective worship have improved since the new system of inspection procedures was introduced in the early 1990s. This is welcome. **We recommend to dioceses that they should agree objectives with schools to raise the standards of teaching, learning and achievement in RE. We further suggest that *all* Church schools whether inspected by Section 10 or Section 23 inspectors should be aspiring to at least a 'Good' rating for the teaching of RE.** The National Society inspection handbook provides clear guidelines on what are to be regarded as acceptable levels of teaching and of learning and achievement for Church of England schools.

**4.13** With good quality religious education and the emphasis given to it in Church schools, **we recommend that all Church secondary schools should expect that pupils should take at least the short course GCSE and preferably the full GCSE in religious studies.** It is encouraging to note that throughout the schools system there has been a major response to the GCSE short course, with 40 per cent of pupils in England as a whole taking a qualification in religious studies at GCSE in 2000. It may be that we are in the middle of a historic change, one that will not only prompt pupils but give extra weight to RE in the thinking of the Teacher Training Agency and the DfEE on Initial Teacher Training. Although we have heard the argument that the absence of a terminal examination gives freedom to teachers and pupils to explore issues that excite their interest, the short course in religious studies should not place burdensome demands on pupils who have been educated in a school which takes the subject seriously, providing it is adequately resourced and over the years has challenged pupils to think critically about religion. The full GCSE should be within the compass of the majority. This should be especially so of Church schools. **We also suggest that Church secondary schools with sixth forms should offer A and AS Level courses in RE, and encourage students to take these courses.**

**4.14** It has been put to us that Church schools should see religious education as a particular specialism, and that they should give the same emphasis to their Christian foundation and Church status as to any other specialist status (e.g. a technology college) that they may acquire. This comment relates to Church secondary schools, but all Church schools should seek to celebrate and enhance their distinctiveness as Christian institutions. To a Church school, religious education and collective worship should be seen as part of an integrated experience, with collective worship acting as an expression of what is taught in many RE lessons. Pupils gain a religious education in its fullest sense in a Church school through good, well-planned and well-organized collective worship, through the example of Christian teachers, and through the quality of RE teaching.

**4.15** What we have said in the preceding paragraphs has implications for the status of RE and RE teachers in all Church schools. We would expect all diocesan boards of education, which have a role in promoting RE and religious worship in **all** schools, to use their influence through Standing Advisory Committees for Religious Education to improve the provision and standard of RE in all schools. **We suggest, as is already the practice in at least some dioceses, that dioceses should seek to offer help to Community schools, on a cost recovery basis, in providing good Religious Education.**

**4.16** The Government has given assurances that the introduction of citizenship into the school curriculum will not result in a reduction in the 5 per cent allocation of time for religious education. We welcome that assurance together with the Government's intention that citizenship should be incorporated into subject syllabuses right across the curriculum. There will certainly be opportunities to relate aspects of Christian teaching to the concept of good citizenship, not least Christ's commandment to love your neighbour as yourself. Respecting and valuing cultural diversity should be a characteristic of all Church schools.

## Voluntary Aided or Voluntary Controlled

**4.17** We set out in Appendix 1 a summary of the characteristics of Voluntary Aided, Voluntary Controlled and Foundation schools. All have their valued place in the Church's provision, but we concentrate here on the first two. At the present time there are nearly 600 more Controlled schools than Aided schools.

**4.18** **Voluntary Controlled and Voluntary Aided schools should rank equally in the care of the Church, and the Church should respond to schools in each category according to their needs.**

**4.19** Voluntary Controlled schools make up a warmly valued part of the community of Church schools, and in many cases may well be indistinguishable from Voluntary Aided schools in their Christian commitment. In rural parts of the country in particular, Voluntary Controlled schools often predominate. As one rural diocese put it in evidence to us, 'most VC schools have strong and active links with their local parishes and, more and more, with the Diocese'. Such schools provide an excellent opportunity for the Church to work in partnership by serving the whole community from the standpoint of Christian service. The value of such schools is immense.

**4.20** The structural benefits of Aided status are outlined in Appendix 1. In brief, this gives a security to the long term Christian character of the school through the structures of the governing body and the role of the governors in shaping the admissions policy. The governing body of an Aided school may also seek evidence of Christian commitment from applications for teaching posts. We recognize the financial implications of any changes to Aided category, but since September 2000 it has been possible for Controlled schools to change their category without reimbursing local authorities for past expenditure. There will of course be future costs arising from a change of category, but in these new circumstances we are glad to note that dioceses have invited governing bodies of Controlled schools to consider whether they want to make a change. From time to time we envisage that dioceses will prompt further reviews.

**4.21** When new Church schools are under consideration, the choice of category will involve close consultation with the local authority. It will be important to proceed by agreement. Financial considerations will be an important factor. For the reasons outlined above we recommend, however, that the **normal preference should be for a Voluntary Aided school, if financial circumstances allow.**

## Partnership with Local Education Authorities

**4.22** A strong and developing partnership between the Church and LEAs is at the heart of our proposals for an increase in the provision of Church schools. The Church and the LEAs have had a long and productive relationship characterized by a spirit of cooperation and genuine debate on the nature and purpose of denominational provision. We wish to emphasize that any development of the Church's provision *is through seeking to proceed in partnership* with the LEAs and with the consent of the local community in response to local needs and opportunities.

**4.23** One Chief Education Officer from an LEA where there has recently been an increase in provision has commented that its aim, and the aim of the diocese, was 'to increase diversity of provision, not to introduce selection by the back door', an issue raised by two of the three teachers' unions who responded to our consultation. In proposing additional Church schools or places in them, that is our aim also. We believe that an expansion of Church schools will contribute to increasing choice and diversity within the overall provision of education, as well as seeking greater parity of provision between Church primary and secondary schools. In particular, the Church has a particular role to play in contributing to the lives and education of children in disadvantaged areas. Discussions on the possibility of increasing provision should therefore be characterized by a spirit of openness and genuine debate on what Church schools can offer to the local community.

**4.24** These discussions should emphasize that Church schools provide a distinctive education based on the Christian notion of community. In this we see the Church working in close partnership with the LEAs, which are also seeking to develop communities. As we have said elsewhere, whilst Church school pupils will experience the Christian ethos and teachings, there should be no intention to proselytize them.

**4.25** The evidence we have received from dioceses and from LEAs shows that the relations between the Church and the local authorities have grown in strength in recent years. This strength is evident across a whole spectrum of activities, for example:

- in cooperation on the Standing Advisory Committees for Religious Education (SACREs) and the development of Agreed Syllabuses;

- in active involvement in the School Organization Committee (evidence shows that a Church representative acts as the Chair in several authorities);

- in the appointment of LEA representatives to some diocesan boards of education or other committees;

- in regular meetings and consultations on matters as diverse as building issues and school inspection and improvement;

- in cooperation on the provision of governor services, training and support;

- in working together on the appointment of headteachers of Church schools;

- in the sharing of technical expertise on a range of issues.

**4.26** We have been impressed by the range of good practice that dioceses and many LEAs have reported in their working relationships, as illustrated below:

> *Examples of good practice provided by LEAs*
> - joint termly meetings between the Chief Education Officer and the diocesan director of education to discuss policy issues and to ensure a consistent approach;
> - termly meetings between the Senior Inspector (or equivalent) responsible for monitoring school performance and diocesan officers to discuss individual Aided and Controlled schools;
> - close partnership in addressing the issues surrounding Church schools in serious weaknesses;
> - close cooperation on buildings issues to consolidate funding arrangements for improving and/or replacing schools.

> *Examples of good practice provided by dioceses*
> 
> - the development of 'partnership agreements' or protocols setting out how the relations between the diocese and LEA are to be conducted;
> 
> - the provision of advice to the LEA on matters relating to small schools, where the Church has a particular depth of experience, especially in rural areas;
> 
> - 'Affiliation Schemes' for Community schools, which provide opportunities for in-service training in RE, collective worship and spiritual and moral development;
> 
> - the buying-in by LEAs of expertise in RE;
> 
> - in one diocese, the two RE advisers are jointly employed by the diocese and LEA. This arrangement provides for a considerable cross-fertilization of ideas, and ensures that a high level of service is available to all schools in the area.

**4.27** Where the Diocese and LEA cover much the same area, the relations between the two are particularly strong. In those areas where a diocese spans several LEAs, the relations are often no less positive, although the relatively sparse resources available to DBEs mean that adequate representation of the Church's interests can demand a large input of time by diocesan directors of education and other officers. By way of illustration, one diocese spans 18 LEAs and appoints over 200 people to various committees.

**4.28** Nevertheless, dioceses have stressed the importance of the Church being adequately represented on local education committees so that the Church's voice is heard in local matters. We believe this is to everyone's benefit because the Church has a concern for the well-being of *all* schools, and because Church schools are a strategically important part of the overall provision within an area and not a separate constituency.

**4.29** We have noted that the strength of the partnership between the Church and LEAs is shown in the willingness of some LEAs to contribute part (or even all) of the Church's capital contribution to a new Aided school, where the case for a new Church school has been accepted as increasing the diversity of educational provision in an area.

**4.30** In a very small number of cases, we have, however, noted that dioceses have reported problems in working with an LEA. This is sometimes the result of different aspirations, or different understandings of the nature of Church schools, or issues surrounding the effects of denominational provision on the 'make-up' of the local community. Such difficulties, if they occur, seem to arise at the Member policy level rather than in the day to day working relations between officers, which we are pleased to say are generally excellent. One diocese has quoted OFSTED's identification of the 'excellent working relationship' between the diocese and LEA. We have also seen that LEAs are often providing a range of practical support to DBEs in inconspicuous ways. In those few cases where it has been difficult to establish good relationships we encourage dioceses to continue to seek to find a basis for understanding and cooperation.

## The views of Chief Education Officers

**4.31** A number of Chief Education Officers and other LEA officers have responded to our interim report issued in July 2000 and to our Consultation Report. In general, their responses have shown a commitment to working in partnership with the Church alongside a willingness to engage in discussions on the provision of Church schools. Their concerns are that potential new Church schools should not upset the local balance of interests; that additional provision should be seen within the context of the local school organization plan; and that new Church schools should be inclusive of the local community.

**4.32** In general, there is support for the Review Group's emphasis on developing the Church's provision in areas of social and economic need (one CEO suggests a particular role for Church schools in helping those with special needs), and for local 'task forces' with LEA involvement, where new schools are being considered.

**4.33** When there have been expressions of concern by the Chief Education Officers they have centred upon the issue of admissions policies. Some have said that the Code of Practice for Admissions (which requires admission policies to be clear and objective) is being contravened by some schools, with a degree of subjectivity being applied to selection, especially where interviews have been used to test religious affiliation. Another said that difficulties sometimes arise when the admission policy appears to discriminate against those for whom there is no realistic alternative, or appears to be used as a means of covert selection. Perhaps it would be a fair comment for us to add that such concerns could apply to all types of school when oversubscription occurs.

**4.34** As we state below, we would expect admissions policies to be clear and objective. We agree that the Church should be responsive to those with special needs.

## Admissions Policies

**4.35** Where the demand for places in a school exceeds the school's capacity, the school's admissions policy becomes an issue of great moment for parents, requiring carefully considered decisions by its governing body. This is true of Community as well as Church schools, but for Church schools a decision on admissions policy uniquely challenges a governing body to decide how it should balance its wish to serve the community in general and its wish to nurture children from Christian homes in their faith.

**4.36** The outcome of the deliberations of the governing body will properly reflect the particular circumstances of the school, and can validly lead to a range of outcomes. We illustrate various scenarios below.

**4.37** For Voluntary Controlled schools, the decisions fall to the local education authority in consultation with the governing body, and we would expect, for example, that for a village school service to the community would predominate in the admissions policy. In our Consultation Report, we suggested, however, that Voluntary Controlled schools should seek agreement that Christian background is among the admissions criteria. We argued that this would allow the school to benefit from the participation of children from Christian homes in the school's defined catchment area, where some degree of choice was required by the level of parental demand, and so help the development and substance of a Christian ethos. Whilst we suggested a quota might be appropriate for such children, we noted that there could be no general rule that fitted all circumstances.

**4.38** Responses to our suggestion have been varied. Some dioceses and LEAs thought that to introduce Christian background or affiliation as an admission criterion for Voluntary Controlled schools would be divisive, potentially excluding local children from the school and restricting parental preference whilst admitting others from a distance. Some commented on the potential funding implications of this in terms of denominational transport, or in terms of the cost to excluded local families who would need to travel farther afield to find a school. It was suggested that seeking Aided status might be a better way of enhancing the Christian distinctiveness of Controlled schools, where such a change of category is supported.

**4.39** On the other hand, a number of dioceses pointed out that denominational preference is already included within the admissions criteria for some or all of their Controlled schools. Practice varies. One diocese has reported that all its Controlled schools include Christian background in their admissions criteria, where 'priority may be given to children whose parents are actual members of the Church of England or Methodist Church'. One diocese has reported looser arrangements representing what parents understand in choosing a Church school. Another diocese suggested it would be legitimate to argue for Church membership as one of the criteria for a new Voluntary Controlled secondary school, if it were the only Church school in a large area, thus reserving some places for children outside the immediate catchment area whose parents specifically request a Church of England school.

**4.40** The range of views expressed and the differences in current practice tell against a recommendation for a uniform national practice of seeking Christian background as one of the admissions criteria in all existing Voluntary Controlled schools. **We recommend, however, that Voluntary Controlled schools should, from time to time, review their distinctiveness as Christian institutions and consider whether their local circumstances allow a legitimate case to be made to the LEA for the inclusion of Christian background within the admissions criteria, providing this does not compromise their tradition and responsibility as a neighbourhood school.**

**4.41** Responses to our consultation have also pointed out that in many rural areas in particular (though not exclusively) Voluntary Aided Church primary schools have historically been the neighbourhood school serving the local community. Such schools may not necessarily fill all the available places through the numbers of children resident in the parish and will therefore attract children from outside for a variety of reasons. In framing their admissions policy, the governors will need to consider the historic foundation of the school and the nature of the local community it serves. Where oversubscription occurs, and this is unlikely to be temporary, the governors should consider whether an enlargement of the school is possible. If this is not possible, or the oversubscription is a temporary occurrence, then the governors will need to consider the priorities for admission, taking into account the potential effects on the ethos of the school and its local tradition. Clear and unambiguous admissions criteria should be set out as required by law, giving an order of priority, and taking into consideration the school's purposes as set out in its original Trust Deed. This may mean giving precedence to the local children irrespective of religious affiliation.

**4.42** To illustrate a different situation in a more urban area, there may occasionally be circumstances in which a more focused admissions policy in favour of Christian background can provide a greater degree of social inclusiveness in a school, especially where the school's catchment area is a generally well-off area. In such circumstances, the admission of a quota of Christian children from a wider area can act as a counterbalance to the selection of children from exclusively affluent backgrounds, especially if the wider community has areas of social and economic deprivation. This comment relates to both Voluntary Aided and Controlled schools.

**4.43** Another situation is that of a Voluntary Aided secondary school in a city, where the demand for places far exceeds the number available because it is the only Church school in a large area. Here, the governing body may justifiably conclude that its task is to nurture Anglican or other Christian children in their faith and to allocate all its resources accordingly. There are other schools in the city to which children can go, and the Church school, as we know from our consultations, may still leave many practising Anglicans unable to find a place.

**4.44** These same consultations have also taught us that even in Church circles such a policy of total commitment to Christian families in the secondary school's wide catchment area may lead to some misgivings on the grounds that the school is not associating with its local community, and not giving an opportunity for non-Christians to experience what it is to learn in a Christian environment. These misgivings are the greater if the local children who do not get in are from disadvantaged sectors of the community whereas the pupils admitted from further away are from the better off districts. The misgivings can be especially strong if there is a racial dimension to this split. There is, therefore, both a community and an ethical reason, linked to the Church's position on poverty and inclusion as set out in paragraph 5.20, for offering a proportion of places for local children. We believe this can be an important factor in winning the hearts and minds of our prospective partners in discussing proposals for additional or expanded Church schools, as well as furthering the mission of the Church. In addition, it may further be argued that the life of the school would be enriched by the admission of some children from other faiths. **We would therefore suggest that some places should be reserved for children of other faiths and of no faith.** This could be achieved either through catchment or quota as appropriate to local circumstances.

**4.45** Where a Church school comes into being as part of a reorganization scheme, or as a 'Fresh Start', it will rightly assume responsibility for an established body of pupils and relate to a particular community. Its future admissions policy will properly be settled by the governors through the normal process which involves circulating draft proposals to other admission authorities who have a chance to object to the adjudicator. We would expect the outcome of the settlement to include Church background amongst the admissions criteria – to an extent that will reflect local circumstances and the category of the school – so that over time its Christian character is developed.

**4.46** Commentators on our Consultation Report have noted that the nature of admissions policies brings into focus the balance between the 'service' and 'nurture' purposes of the Church in education. How that balance is determined will reflect the category of the school, its ethos, history and tradition, and local circumstances. In general, **we recommend that new Voluntary Aided Church schools should aim to allocate 'open' and 'foundation' places, the ratio between the two reflecting the school's particular circumstances, whilst ensuring strong distinctiveness and diversity. A degree of flexibility may be required in the allocation.**

**4.47** Whatever the particular circumstances, we would recommend that:

- **Voluntary Aided schools must comply with the Code of Practice on School Admissions, ensuring that admission criteria are clear, objective and fair.**

- **The governing body should set out the geographical area from which admissions will be given priority.**

- **Voluntary Aided schools should aim to offer a number of places as a high priority to children with special educational or medical needs, as representing the Church's commitment to those most in need.**

- **All Church schools should consider how they are responding to the changing needs of the local community.**

- **In any new primary and secondary schools it should be the policy to establish within measurable time – if it is not possible from the outset – at least a substantial minority of pupils with a Christian background.**

- **In particular, the aim over time in new Voluntary Aided schools should be to achieve an appropriate balance of 'open' and 'foundation' places, sufficient to ensure that the school is a distinctively Christian institution whilst remaining grounded in the local community in all its diversity.**

- **All dioceses should adopt the policy already employed by many dioceses of offering guidance to schools on their admissions policy.**

## The place of an ecumenical approach to education

**4.48** Happily, the keen interdenominational rivalry that was so evident in the creation of Church schools in the nineteenth century is no longer an issue, although the different Christian Churches have usually promoted schools serving one denomination. There are, however, already good examples of collaborative working between denominations in existing schools, and in the development of new schools.

**4.49** In extending provision as we propose at both primary and secondary levels, and especially in areas of deprivation where an existing school might be finding a new future as a Church school, the challenges may be very great. The purposes of the Churches may well be best served both in responding to the needs of the community and in giving a strongly based Christian dimension to the life of the school by creative solutions involving an ecumenical approach drawing on the resources and commitment of two or more Churches or denominations. This is as relevant to primary as to secondary provision.

**4.50** In particular, in considering the development of new Church schools, the aim should be to avoid destabilizing any existing denominational provision, by recognizing the presence and interests of the existing school. There may well be circumstances where, in the light of the current provision, it would be in the interests of the Churches to work together, in order to ensure the long-term continuity of a strong Christian presence.

**4.51** When opportunities for a new Voluntary school arise, events may move quickly and unless there has been preparatory dialogue about joint schools beforehand the pressure of events may rule out a joint proposal.

**4.52** We recommend that in appropriate circumstances the Church should welcome an ecumenical approach to new schools, actively fostering a will for the denominations to work together, and that dioceses should through continuing contact with other denominations be continually alert to opportunities.

## Independent Anglican schools

**4.53** There are around 500 independent schools which claim explicitly to be Anglican foundations, with over a hundred more which are Anglican by association, either from historical circumstance or through the maintenance of an Anglican chaplaincy. Of these, at least 250 are secondary schools. These schools are an important element in the community of schools that have a Christian foundation. (The distribution of independent secondary schools that have an Anglican foundation is shown in Appendix 2.)

**4.54** Where the link to the Church is strong, these schools are more secure in their distinctive Anglican identity. The cathedral and collegiate foundations and the independent schools belonging to or associated with the Woodard Corporation are amongst these. Many other independent schools have worked hard to maintain their identity as Anglican foundations, giving emphasis to worship and chaplaincy and to their Christian ethos.

**4.55** The evidence we have received, however, suggests that in many independent schools the Anglican foundation has been attenuated, either as a result of the weakening of links between the school and the diocese, or through commercial and external pressures. In many of these schools, the selection of pupils and staff is being made increasingly without reference to the Anglican nature of the school. The Church itself has sometimes been ambivalent in its attitude towards independent education. The current Review therefore offers the opportunity to reappraise the place of Anglican independent schools within the Church's ministry.

**4.56** If we believe that Church schools stand at the centre of the Church's mission to the nation, then this belief must embrace the Anglican independent schools as well. There is a real need for the Church to re-engage with these schools, fostering a sense of belonging, and working with them towards a more explicit recognition of both ordained and lay ministry in these schools, through chaplaincy, governance and the education they offer. For their part, these independent schools should be encouraged to re-evaluate their own identities, to make them explicit in their signage, to develop links with dioceses and maintained Church schools, and to strengthen their distinctiveness.

**4.57** To that end we make the following recommendations:

- The bishops should foster a sense of shared community between the Anglican independent schools and the maintained Church schools in their dioceses by holding, for example, an annual meeting with heads to discuss issues of shared concern and to foster the development of bilateral relationships between independent and maintained schools. This would be with a view to identifying opportunities to enhance the work of each other, for example, in sharing scarce teaching resources, broadening the experience of staff, developing approaches to religious education, worship and chaplaincy, short pupil exchanges, and shared cultural activities – music, art and drama.

- The independent schools in a diocese should be invited to propose a member for the Diocesan Board of Education (DBE), and reciprocally bishops should canvass the possibility of a DBE representative or other nominee of the bishop being invited to become a member of the governing body of independent secondary schools.

- The Church should always be mindful of the independent Anglican schools in its stewardship at national and diocesan level, and in its activities, e.g. in annual services of dedication for Christian teachers and invitations to educational events. The Church should consciously pursue a policy of inclusiveness.

- The Anglican independent schools should be encouraged to engage with the resources available from the National Society on the Character of Anglican Schools in the Independent Sector, as a supplement to material provided by the Independent Schools Inspectorate.

**4.58** To sum up, as part of our advocacy of one cohering Church community in which each part seeks to work with and for the others, we advocate a proactive policy of partnership between the maintained and independent schools. The purpose of this partnership is to nourish the Christian identity and the quality of education and school life the schools offer. The independent schools have much to offer, not least in their sense of community. We remember well hearing from staff and pupils at one we visited, 'This is a friendly place: we care for one another.' We concurred with that statement. This development of the capacity for caring and community is an important element in education, which a school with boarding students in particular has an opportunity to understand and live. In a different way, through the wide spectrum of social backgrounds in many maintained schools there is the opportunity to learn the meaning of community in another distinctive way. In both, the basis of community is the shared aspiration of the Christian commandment to love one another.

## Conclusion

**4.59** The guidelines we offer for consideration in this and the preceding chapter, which need to be considered as a whole, represent a confirmation that the Church should seek to serve children of all faiths and none.

**4.60** In all circumstances we would recommend that Church schools must be distinctively places where the Christian faith is alive and practised. Church schools will seek to offer excellence in education, and in so doing they will above all be concerned to develop the whole human being through the practice of the Christian faith.

**4.61** To facilitate responsiveness in admissions to the criteria discussed earlier in this chapter, and to facilitate the engagement of a substantial core of Christian teachers who together will give the school its Christian character, we see advantage, where that is possible and affordable, for additional schools to be in the Voluntary Aided category.

**4.62** We warmly endorse the practice of partnership between the Church and Government at national level and have been glad to see the way in which partnership between the Church and local government has been developing in recent years. We see partnerships in which the Church offers its distinctive contribution to communities as a valuable and continuing element in the Church's practice in education.

*chapter 5*
# Proposals for increased provision

**5.1** The present provision of Church schools is largely the product of the huge commitment made by the Church to providing elementary education for the poor in the nineteenth century and different decisions taken by individual dioceses over many decades. It does not reflect the needs of a Church that sees its schools at the centre of its mission to the nation. Against that criterion, it is seriously lacking.

**5.2** The current provision is characterized by:

- a major imbalance between the provision of places in primary as opposed to secondary schools, i.e. in 2000:

    774,000 primary places

    150,000 secondary places

    which means that taking a national overview only one in five children in a Church primary school can be offered a place in a Church secondary school, although there are considerable disparities in access from place to place;

- large discrepancies in provision between dioceses, with six dioceses having no secondary schools;

- under-representation in the suburbs and especially in outer London;

- more Voluntary Controlled than Voluntary Aided schools: 2,638 Controlled as against 2,058 Aided, with major differences between one diocese and another.

**5.3** In Appendix 2 we offer an analysis of the current provision of Church schools by diocese.

**5.4** We do not wish to argue for uniformity. Decisions have been taken in the past for good reasons, and often there is no one course that is better than another in all respects. But such past decisions taken for good reasons do not mean that they are still the best for the present time. The present is a time when society is more secular than ever before, but partly because of this many parents are seeking education for their children in Church schools. The main national political parties are showing goodwill to a constructive partnership with the Churches in the provision of education. At local level, too, many authorities are welcoming to Church schools and working in a spirit of partnership in the local structures established under the School Standards and Framework Act 1998. This, therefore, is a time of welcome to the Church in education, and a time when the Church schools offer the gospel to a large number, young and old, who would not choose to attend formal church services.

**5.5** It is not simply in the secondary sector that there is a large imbalance in provision between dioceses. By applying a demographic analysis to the number of Church schools, we have found that our primary provision varies markedly from one diocese to another, with a diocese at one extreme having only about one tenth of the provision of the best provided diocese. That represents a large difference in provision. Dioceses that are particularly underprovided in primary schools are the densely populated urban dioceses in the south east and the industrial north and midlands. These have been the areas of rapid population growth and housing development in the nineteenth and twentieth centuries. Suburban areas are generally underprovided. For some of those dioceses to aim for the national average provision for Church primary schools would mean doubling or even tripling their primary provision. That is not feasible even as a long-term possibility for those dioceses, but the imbalances in primary provision should prompt some dioceses with below average provision to seek an increase. We already know of schemes being undertaken by some dioceses to do this.

**5.6** **Accordingly, we recommend that dioceses should review their existing primary provision with a view to improving it in the light of identified local need as a long-term aim where the present provision is seen to be very low.** We suggest that dioceses should use the well-known national average statistic that one in four primary schools is a Church of England school (educating about one in five pupils) as a possible reference point for beginning to identify future need. Statistics are of course no more than a starting point, but they are useful in suggesting areas for examination.

**5.7** It is important to say here in relation to our recommendations for an increase in both primary and secondary provision, that the Church is not in the business of creating surplus places by displacing other schools that are already providing valued service to the community. Its task is to respond to need and to work by agreement with partners at local level. It must proceed by consent, recognizing that other providers will have their own legitimate aspirations.

## Church of England secondary schools: an invitation and a challenge

**5.8** In our July 2000 interim report to the Archbishops' Council, we commented on the big disparity in provision between our primary and secondary schools, and drew attention to the large geographical gaps in our secondary provision. In large areas of England and Wales, it is not possible to attend a Church of England (or Church in Wales) secondary school simply because there are none there. We invited all dioceses to consider the feasibility of increasing their secondary provision by the equivalent of two schools (or three if the diocese had no secondary school or only one) over the next five years. That would mean the equivalent of 100 additional Church of England secondary schools if our challenge could eventually be realized across all the dioceses. That, in itself, would only go a modest part of the way to reducing the current mismatch of 625,000 places between our primary and secondary schools. Our demographic analysis has shown that even to go half-way towards parity of provision with our primary schools, we would need an additional 250 secondary schools. We made this observation in order to illustrate the need to improve the current balance of provision.

**5.9** In making our recommendation in July 2000, we were conscious of the unsatisfied demand for places in many Church of England secondary schools. A recent survey we carried out with the cooperation of the Association of Anglican Secondary School Headteachers confirmed large levels of over subscription for places at many Church secondary schools. Some 80 secondary schools took part in our survey. In these schools the average level of over subscription in 2000 was 1.6 applicants per Year 7 place as compared with 1.3 applicants per place in 1996 (with a steadily increasing ratio in the intervening years).

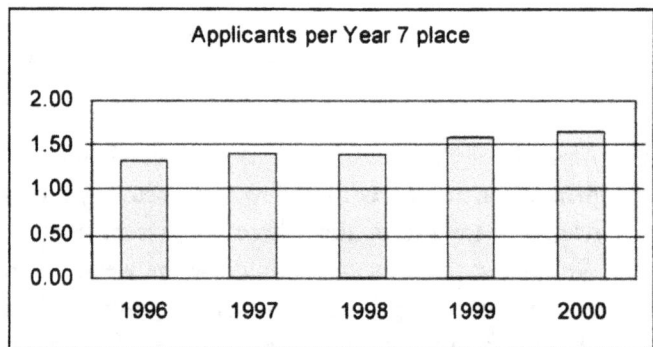

**5.10** We know that a number of dioceses are already making plans to increase their secondary school provision, or have long-term aspirations to do so. During the course of our work a number of new Church schools have been announced and two new Church of England secondary schools have opened in the Diocese of Bradford, which together provide places for some 2,500 pupils. The challenges of such an ambitious programme of expansion as has been undertaken in Bradford are very great indeed and will continue into the future, but this example indicates what can be achieved where there is strong local support from the community, a strong and creative partnership with the local education authority, and a commitment to inclusiveness.

**5.11** In their consultation responses, dioceses have shown that they see differing scope and opportunities for the development of secondary provision. Whilst some are keen to expand provision and are actively engaged in discussion with local partners, some others have pointed out that their capacity for expansion is constrained by local demographic factors, and have pointed to the fact of falling rolls and increasing numbers of surplus places in their areas generally. Some dioceses have said that they would prefer to consolidate and strengthen their existing provision before attempting any expansion, and to develop better links with Community or independent schools. Many dioceses have said that while they want to increase secondary provision they see it as a longer-term process than the five years we suggested last summer. Others have pointed out that their limited financial resources are an inhibiting factor to expansion.

**5.12** Since dioceses made their responses to the Consultation Report the Government has published its Green Paper on Schools (CM 5050) which widens the scope for faith communities in education, and proposes a reduction in the governors' capital contribution to the costs of Voluntary Aided schools from 15 to 10 per cent. This will enlarge the opportunities for increased Church provision in partnership with LEAs, and reduce the financial obstacles to additional provision. We have noted elsewhere that LEAs are sometimes willing to contribute to capital costs and, of course, where a Voluntary Controlled school is concerned, no capital contribution is required. Some funding for Church schools is available under the Private Finance Initiative (see 5.25). With the reduction in the capital contribution to 10 per cent, the option of Voluntary Controlled schools and the possibility of some assistance from national fundraising, we hope that dioceses will see the financial dimension of increased provision to be somewhat less daunting. But funding will remain an issue with many dioceses and we therefore propose a national fundraising initiative (see 5.22–5.31).

**5.13** Some other constraints to expansion are very real. Dioceses can only proceed where there is opportunity, and the national need for additional secondary schools will be modest: secondary school pupil numbers are expected to peak in 2004 and thereafter to decline to their present numbers by 2011. The provision of additional Church schools and the enlargement of existing Church schools will therefore depend very much on local schemes of school reorganization, responses to schools in difficulty, and on detailed discussions with LEAs and Schools Organization Committees on Church proposals.

**5.14** Nevertheless, with increasing demand from parents for places in Church schools, the goodwill of the main national political parties and many local educational authorities, and the clear need to expand secondary provision if Church schools are indeed to be at the centre of the Church's mission to **the whole** nation, we recommend that either through additional schools or through the expansion of existing Church schools, the Church should aim to increase its secondary provision by the equivalent of 100 schools. This would mean a rise in the Church's current share of secondary places from approximately 5 per cent to 8 per cent (assuming an average secondary school to have around 900 places) but would still leave a high imbalance between secondary and primary provision. We envisage that new schools established because of basic need will only be a small proportion of the 100 schools. Most will, therefore, have to come about as a result of school reorganizations or partnerships or where the Church is invited to take on a struggling Community school (see our proposal in 5.35–5.37).

> *As an example of a Community school that has become a Church school, the Trinity School (Diocese of Rochester) grew out of the Picardy School, a mixed secondary modern school operating on two sites in the 'Picardy' area of Belvedere. Of the school's translation to Church of England Voluntary Aided status, achieved with the full support of the LEA, its first headteacher, Mr Ray Slade, has written:*
>
> > 'The concept was right. A Church of England School, with Christian values was just what was needed in our locality.
> >
> > The support given by the governors, by the diocese through the school's voluntary aided status and by the wider community has been magnificent.
> >
> > The splendid and sustained hard work of the staff, teaching and non-teaching has been essential – without that no school can succeed.
> >
> > But above all, Trinity School is God's work. His handiwork sustained by the prayers of his people.'

**5.15** Assuming responsibility for a Community school that has been in difficulty will be a demanding exercise. It should only be considered where the Church has the resources to ensure effective management of the transition and the leadership necessary to develop a new sense of purpose and achievement within the school. We would emphasize that strong support for the headteacher of a new school during the first few years is essential, especially when the Church is assuming responsibility for a school community that has previously been in difficulty. There are already examples of good practice, where the Church has helped in such situations, such as the foundation partnership between a well-established Church school and a new Church school on the model of St Peter's Collegiate School and the King's School in Wolverhampton. The growing number of 'Beacon' schools may also be in a position to give help and support to others.

**5.16** In sustaining our earlier recommendation of the equivalent of 100 additional Church secondary schools we recognize that our initial proposal of two additional schools for most dioceses and three where the diocese has no secondary school, or only one, needs to be refined in the light of a detailed analysis of existing provision in relation to school populations. For some dioceses which already have two or more secondary schools, the number of Church school places in relation to population may nevertheless be notably limited, and an increase in provision of one, two, or more schools would be desirable. For others, where provision is strong and generally well balanced, an increase of one, or some expansion of existing schools, may be a measure of what is desirable in relation to an overall figure of 100 additional schools.

**5.17** As to the timescale, this is only partly in the Church's hands. There are issues of opportunity, finance, school leadership, and diocesan resource. Whilst the proposals in the February Government Green Paper are certainly helpful, and there is much that the Church itself can do over time to address issues on the lines suggested in this report, we recognize that a five-year timescale was extremely ambitious. In responding to the Resolution of the

General Synod as set out in our terms of reference, we thought it right to challenge the Church and to invite it to be ambitious. Rather than five years, however, we have concluded it would be more realistic to be thinking of, say, seven to eight years, albeit with dioceses setting themselves objectives for the next five years.

**5.18** Within the total, we include **City Academies,** two of which so far commissioned have a Church of England involvement. We encourage the Church in partnership with the local community to seek actively to increase the number subject to consultation with the local authorities, and to support fundraising to that end. Our consultation has shown evidence of active interest and activity in several dioceses. We would also encourage dioceses to respond to initiatives of the kind canvassed in the Green Paper for Voluntary Sector Sponsors to take responsibility for a school under the terms of a fixed term renewable contract (CM 5050 paras 4.23–4.24) and the Church nationally to ensure that it has the organizational structure to engage proactively in them. **We see some of the strong existing Church secondary schools providing opportunities for helpful partnership with Community schools that may come into the Church community in response to the Green Paper proposals** (see 5.32–5.37). Whilst not included in the total of 100 we welcome affiliation arrangements with Community schools of the kind introduced in the Guildford Diocese.

**5.19** There may also be opportunities for involvement in post-16 provision and partnerships with Learning and Skills Councils and other community-based learning programmes.

**5.20** In considering additional provision, **we invite dioceses to have an especial commitment to expanding provision in areas of economic and social hardship.** It was the call to serve the poor that took the Church so magnificently into education in the nineteenth century. Today, the Church is still committed to serving those in the most deprived areas of society, in the inner city and in rural areas where deprivation may be less visible because it is dispersed but is no less real. **It should be an especial care of the Church today to renew that commitment to those who have least in life; to the children who are most likely to lose out in the life ahead of them.** We live in a society where the gap between the affluent and the poor causes much concern, and where there is a very real risk that the children of the poor are destined to remain poor, unless their talents can be nourished and their aspirations raised through an education that is excellent and that gives real hope. This is an issue that the Church would do well to see as a mission in which it must engage. We so recommend.

## A national policy

**5.21** To sum up, we recommend that the Church should:

- at the primary level, increase provision where it is most evidently lacking;

- aim to increase secondary places, whether by the expansion of existing Church schools or through additional Church schools (including transfers from the Community sector), by the equivalent of 100 schools over the next seven to eight years;

- consider within each diocese what can be achieved over the next five years, and to roll forward its thinking annually by a further year;
- in increasing provision, see it as part of its special mission to serve the most disadvantaged in society, and children with special educational needs;
- foster an ecumenical approach where this is appropriate and be careful not to destabilize existing faith schools;
- engage in national fundraising;

We suggest that the Archbishops' Council should review progress annually.

## Financial resource implications: a national appeal

**5.22** Where a new Voluntary Aided school is created, the governors have been required to contribute 15 per cent of the capital cost. As we said earlier, the February Green Paper proposes to decrease the 15 per cent to 10 per cent. That is both welcome and very relevant to the Church's ability to increase provision. Even so, with the addition of Value Added Tax (which applies to Voluntary Aided schools but not to schools funded entirely by the local authority) for a new Church Voluntary Aided school the contribution could be in the range of say £1.25 million to £1.8 million. For new primary schools the sums are smaller but still material. Where an existing secondary school passes to the Church, the sum required may also be very much smaller and these are likely to constitute the main opportunities for increasing provision. Without question the financial resourcing of additional provision will be a big factor in the consideration of our recommendations, the more especially as there will be calls on finance for the continuing process of repair and improvement of existing schools. Dioceses will also have to resource the revenue costs of setting up additional schools and consider the cost of Church contributions to their long-term maintenance.

**5.23** The evidence we have received from dioceses suggests that only a limited number of them would have the capital resources to finance one new Voluntary Aided secondary school. In a very small number of cases a diocese might be able to finance two. This reflects the uneven distribution of diocesan trust funds. We do not suggest a pooling of these funds since no diocese is excessively resourced in relation to its needs.

**5.24** However, the financial dimension need not be as daunting as the figures above may suggest. We have found that the cost of a new Voluntary Aided school is a matter for negotiation case by case. Sometimes, the capital contribution can be met in part by developers from 'development gain'. In other cases, the local authority may be willing to contribute very substantially towards the capital contribution. For City Academies, which we envisage being part of the response to our proposals for additional secondary schools, the Government made clear that it saw part of the envisaged capital contribution coming from a donor, as has happened in the two announced in 2000 in which the Church is a partner. Where the Church takes on responsibility for an existing Community school, for example as part of a reorganization scheme, any capital sum involved will be far less than that for a new school. We envisage that the great majority of the additional secondary places we canvass will in fact come from the Church taking responsibility, in agreement with an LEA, for an existing school. In the case of a Voluntary Controlled school, the capital costs are met by the LEA, and if finance is lacking, designation as a Voluntary Controlled school can be the way forward.

**5.25** It is also relevant to note that the provisions of the 1944 Education Act for loans towards the capital costs of new schools have been continued in force by the School Standards and Framework Act 1998. There are also opportunities under the Private Finance Initiative (PFI), which enables governing bodies to meet their percentage contribution to capital costs over the period of the contract. There are PFI credits available from the DfEE for building work in Church of England Voluntary Aided schools. The National Society is currently working on a bid for possible projects.

**5.26** There will nevertheless be a need for new money if the Church can contemplate the provision of the equivalent of an extra 100 secondary schools. This will be needed to help dioceses make a contribution to capital costs, when the need arises, and to support dioceses in carrying forward the work needed to negotiate provision and support the new schools' headteachers in their initial year.

## Fundraising

**5.27** Taking first the resourcing of the diocesan effort, the evidence we have received from dioceses and from the Church of England Board of Education and National Society Council has suggested that dioceses, in general, have small education teams and do not have the human resources available to undertake a programme of school expansion. In our Consultation Report, we suggested the establishment of regionally based task forces to assist dioceses in this task. These task forces would draw in expertise from a variety of sources – dioceses, local education authorities and others – and would be tailored to the individual needs of a project. We envisage that these task forces would provide back-up to the mechanism outlined in paragraph 5.34 for assessing the future of a struggling Community school, and assist in the work required to establish a new Church school. A number of dioceses have welcomed this suggestion, which is intended to share experience and good practice and to supplement dioceses' own staffing resources in response to perceived needs, whilst dioceses would themselves remain in overall management control of the project being undertaken. We envisage that such task forces could help in the project management area or in preparing bids for new schools such as City Academies, or in the much-needed support for the headteacher of a new Church school during the start-up phase. **We recommend that such task forces would have a nationally co-ordinated dimension in order to maintain the national overview of development and to provide access to national expertise. We also recommend that dioceses should review their existing support for their boards of education and that the resources of the Church of England Board of Education and National Society should be strengthened in response to this report.** We estimate that over a period of say seven to eight years the additional costs could amount to £6 million.

**5.28** Turning to the capital contribution needed to supplement diocesan resources, we find very great uncertainties, for the sums required will turn on the balance of Voluntary Controlled as opposed to Voluntary Aided schools, the proportion of new as opposed to continuing schools and the extent to which the LEAs contribute or share 'development gains' from developers. Any estimate therefore could prove wildly wrong, but, to attempt some indication of the scale of an appeal, after including the £6 million revenue costs and assuming that the Church will be largely taking responsibility for existing schools rather than building new ones, **the total (excluding City Academies) could be in the order of £20 million** to be raised over a period of seven years. It could be decidedly more.

**5.29** City Academies have not been included in this figure of £20 million because, with the higher required level of financial contribution (20 per cent rather than 10 per cent) and the relatively modest number of them, each will be a special case to be tackled individually through a donor or donors able to contribute sums ranging from say £0.7 million for improving an existing school to £2.5 million for a new school.

**5.30** While we suggest the funding of City Academies needs an individual approach to financing, it will assist progress if there can be pump priming from the national fund and it would be desirable, if possible, to set the national appeal at £25 million. If good progress is to be made the whole fundraising effort needs to be led, managed and coordinated at national level. To that end we recommend the creation of an executive appeals group of people of standing, suitably supported, possibly by a professional fundraiser, to lead and develop an appeal for £25 million over seven years and to assist in raising funds for individual City Academies, where these are part of a locally agreed solution (see 5.18).

**5.31** We see the appeal seeking support from individual benefactors, charitable foundations, trusts, and corporations (as opposed to an appeal to the parishes). Appeals to such bodies are often most successful if they relate to a particular project in a particular locality. We suggest that an important part of the task of the national committee, in consultation with diocesan bishops, would therefore be to identify potential donors across the dioceses who might be brought together at diocesan level.

## Developing our provision in partnership with LEAs and Government

**5.32** In its Green Paper, Schools Building on Success, published in February 2001, the Government welcomed our proposal to increase the number of Church schools, particularly at the secondary level, and extended this welcome to all the churches and other faith groups. As we have already noted, the Green Paper has proposed a reduction in the contribution paid by the governors and promoters of Voluntary Aided schools towards the capital costs of a new school from 15 per cent to 10 per cent. The Green Paper also included a proposal to develop a model that would enable a private or voluntary sector sponsor to take responsibility for a weak or failing school on a renewable fixed term contract of five to seven years. There was also a proposal to extend this option to successful schools that wish, for example, to develop a more distinct identity.

**5.33** We welcome this renewed commitment to a developing partnership between the state and faith-based schools, and in response have invited the Government to consider our own proposal for developing the provision of Church and other faith schools. Our own proposal emphasizes our partnership with local education authorities in meeting the educational needs of the community, and in the case of a failing Community school the possibility of the school becoming a Church school as one option for addressing failure.

**5.34** Our proposal is as follows:

- In appropriate circumstances, say after a secondary school had been placed in special measures or serious weakness following its OFSTED inspection, or where a secondary school was struggling, the LEA would enter into dialogue with the local faith groups to establish which group or groups might have an interest. The Church of England would be an obvious partner with which to begin discussions since its schools serve the wider community. At this stage, it would also be perfectly possible to begin a dialogue between groups with a view to establishing an ecumenical school.

- Assuming that a Church of England school would be considered, the LEA and the Diocese would each appoint a suitably experienced individual. Working together, these two individuals would then form an assessment of the options for the school. Those appointed might be eligible for funding from the Standards Fund, but funding could come jointly from the diocese, LEA and DfEE.

- The LEA would retain responsibility for assessing the possible closure of the school, taking into account the availability of other places in the area.

- Acting in a consultancy role, the two individuals would perform an assessment of the efficacy of a 'Fresh Start' (FS) kind of arrangement, in consultation with the diocese and LEA. Such arrangements would envisage two possible categories: (a) FS Community school; (b) FS Voluntary school.

**5.35** Where it involved a change from a Community to a Voluntary school, the features of a FS Voluntary School would be as follows:

1. There would be a presumption in favour of it wherever there was no secondary school with a religious character in the geographical area.

2. The two individuals appointed by the diocese and LEA would consult parents and the local community (including parishes) about whether they supported the school changing from a Community to a Voluntary Church school. Assuming that such support was forthcoming, the following points would apply.

3. The ethos and practice of the new school would be distinctively Christian, but it would not proselytize.

4. Parents would be informed of the implications of the change to a Church school.

5. All existing pupils would be guaranteed a place in the new school and would be expected to stay. The LEA would use its best endeavours to find alternative schools for pupils whose parents did not wish them to continue their education in a Church school.

6. It would have been made clear during the consultation process that the new school's Admissions Policy would be structured so as to keep faith with the local community and the historic tradition of the school as the local provider. This would require a clearly defined priority zone for the local children. However, it would be possible for additional Christian children from outside the priority zone to gain admission if there was a degree of undersubscription. In the event of an ecumenical venture, some flexibility might be required in the admission arrangements so as to achieve the desired balance in admissions.

7. It could be accepted that TUPE (Transfer of Undertakings (Protection of Employment)) would apply since the employer would change. However, the LEA would use its best endeavours to find alternative places for staff who did not wish to work in a Church school.

8. The school site would be transferred to the new Church school's trustees and held on trust, with a reverter to the LEA in the event of the school closing.

**5.36** It should be possible, along the lines of the analogy with the Government's proposed 'Contract' schools, for a successful Community school to consider becoming a Voluntary Church school, where the school wishes it. In these circumstances, similar considerations would apply to those outlined above, with the normal statutory procedure for closure and for opening a new school applying. Existing pupils would be guaranteed places or given an alternative, with the Admissions Policy providing similar safeguards to the local children as in the case of a failing Community school that had been transferred to the Church.

**5.37** In the case of both a struggling or successful Community school that could be transferred to the Church, the School Organization Committee would have a duty to consider such a proposal, with appropriate guidance being given. In the event of a disagreement on the feasibility of such an option, the matter would be referred to the adjudicator, who would also need guidance on such proposals. However, any such proposal should have been thoroughly investigated and discussed between the LEA and the Diocese before its referral to the School Organization Committee.

*chapter 6*
# Teachers, teachers, teachers

**6.1** If in thirty years' time a committee like the present one is appointed to advise on Church schools we hope, in reflecting on the first thirty years of the twenty-first century, it will be able to say something like, 'the Church's realization that the whole future of its schools was dependent upon its ability to recruit Christian teachers, retain them in the profession, and develop them for leadership positions in schools – and its response to that realization – was the foundation of the growing strength and the esteem Church schools have achieved with all sections of society over the last thirty years'.

**6.2** In education, every study should begin and end with pupils and teachers and this is especially so of the Church at this time, when society is showing that it would welcome more opportunities for children to go to Church schools. At the same time, in an increasingly secular society the seedbed of young Christians from whom Christian teachers can be drawn needs to be nourished. Unless the Church can act successfully to find the teachers needed for the schools it already has, and for the increased provision recommended in our report, nothing will be achieved. Without an effective programme of action, a lack of Christian teachers could set everything at naught.

**6.3** The long-term provision of Christian teachers and especially of head and deputy headteachers must therefore be the principal concern of this Review Group.

## Three immediate issues for action by the Church

**6.4** Within the wider field of action that is needed, we identify three issues that are especially urgent and requiring action. They are:

### (a) To raise the respect for and the morale of teachers in our society

**6.5** Teachers feel undervalued in our society. The respect that was once theirs is often hard won and too often lacking. Where this is so, it undermines their authority and effectiveness in the classroom and their standing with parents. It bears directly on the willingness of people to enter the profession and on the retention of those already in the profession. This is an issue for the whole nation. But it is one that can and should be tackled by the Church. Church schools should stand out as places where teachers and other staff are valued and respected. The headteacher should be able to look to the parish church as a source of unfailing support and encouragement. Governors, particularly the Chair, as well as the parish and the diocese all have a part to play; it is their business to know the headteacher, to help, to sustain and to encourage.

**6.6** Many governors are selected and appointed by the Church at parish or diocesan level. **The Church needs to recognize that to be a school governor is one of the most important roles that a Church member can take.** It is good if some, or at least one, of the school governors is also a member of the PCC, and the role of governor should be recognized as being at least as important as membership of the PCC. For most, the time taken to be a governor will be much greater than the time taken to be a member of the PCC. The role of Chair is comparable to being a churchwarden.

**6.7** As we say in Chapter 8 governors have a key role in the appointment of headteachers and of other school staff. Having appointed staff, and got to know them in the process, governors need to build on that acquaintance and show how much staff are valued for themselves as people as well as for their professional work. **Governors should see it as a core part of their role to relate personally to all members of staff individually.** In a large school this may need to be done on a departmental or some other suitable basis. All staff should feel that at least one governor makes time to talk and listen to them and seeks to help them.

**6.8** **Governors also have an important task with parents.** They should do everything they can to present the good work of the school to the parents and, in particular, to help parents understand how much the teachers and other staff are doing to ensure the well-being and progress of their children. **Parents need to be encouraged by governors to show their appreciation of the work of teachers by expressing thanks and showing that they value the care which teachers are taking to help the children.** Such action is important in raising the standing of teachers in the eyes of the community and hence in helping to raise their morale.

**6.9** Teachers are potentially the best, or most critical, ambassadors for their own profession. Unless they feel valued they will not encourage their own pupils, friends and Church members to enter the profession. If they feel valued they will be the best people to encourage some of the very large number of qualified teachers, many of them practising Christians, who are not currently teaching, to return to the profession. Sadly, at present many do not feel able to recommend the profession in this way.

**6.10** **In the interests of high standards, churches have a duty to support teachers in whatever way possible.** In particular, Church members should show that they value what teachers do. They should show an interest in the teachers as people as well as in the schools as institutions. **Headteachers, or other suitable teachers, should have the opportunity to talk regularly to PCCs. Indeed, where possible, the headteacher should be a valued member of the PCC. Parish magazines should contain news of the schools in the parish and should seek to show the good work of the staff.**

**6.11** **We counsel that Church members, school governors and headteachers should keep in touch with teachers from the school who have left the profession before retirement,** whether to have a family or to try some other apparently more attractive job. If they feel valued they are more likely to consider returning to the school. To this end, schools should make sure that such people continue to be invited to events, special services and other functions if they are still living in the area and keep them informed of the progress of the school and their former pupils.

**6.12** Underpinning all this is a triangular relationship between incumbent, parish and school (children and parents) which we illustrated in Chapter 1. This is what is needed if Church schools are to be at the heart of the Church's mission to the nation.

**6.13** The dioceses have a key part to play in caring for staff. Gatherings for new headteachers and for new staff, preferably on a residential basis, are much valued because they offer an opportunity to establish a network of people sharing the same kind of experience. We refer in Chapter 7 to the helpful and important role of the clergy in schools.

**6.14** The headteacher has, of course, a central role in developing and fostering respect for teachers and, if need be, in structuring the kind of action by the governing body outlined above. Fostering respect for teachers also means that where there is weakness in teaching performance the headteacher and, where necessary, the governing body should be ready to put matters right, first by identifying the causes, and then by taking whatever action is needed to re-establish high standards.

**6.15** Action on the lines we have illustrated in this section is crucial at this time to the Church's ability to attract and retain Christian teachers, to the quality of the work of the teachers themselves, and to the achievement of the schools. Teachers who know themselves to be highly respected and valued will moreover be more likely to build up self respect and self-confidence among the pupils they teach. **We therefore strongly urge the Church at all levels, and the governing bodies in particular, to commit themselves to the practices described in this section, which are aimed to raise respect for, and foster a genuine sense of being valued in the teaching profession. We recommend accordingly.**

### (b) To develop a corps of heads and other school leaders

**6.16** If the action we have proposed to increase the number of Church schools is to succeed, the Church will need to find the headteachers and senior staff who can provide the leadership to make them places of Christian nurture and 'successful schools' in the conventional usage of words. **It must be seen as a major concern of the Church at national and diocesan level to identify, develop and recruit committed leaders from Christian teachers in all schools.** The challenge to these future heads will be especially great when the Church assumes responsibility for a school in difficulty. Without the right Christian leaders the Church cannot responsibly accept the challenge of such schools.

**6.17** Of course, this issue extends beyond the need for heads and other leaders for new schools. Its successful resolution will bear directly on the ability of Church schools to recruit the Christian teachers they need to give them their distinctive character. It is the long-term issue, more than any other, upon which the future of Church schools depends.

**6.18** We would recommend that the response must include action now to identify on a national basis, diocese by diocese, Christian teachers of all ages, young and old, who have the potential to provide the necessary leadership. The dioceses must see that these teachers have the in-service development needed to move on to senior positions. This preparation will encompass training in the practice of management in schools and the development of their knowledge of Church schools and religious education. For the former, we welcome initiatives taken by the Association of Anglican Secondary School Headteachers. The new National College for School Leadership and other regional leadership centres also provide valuable opportunities, and we welcome the appointment of the head of a Church school to the governing body of the former. Modules need to be developed by the National College for School Leadership that are particularly relevant to the leadership of Church schools. It is of particular concern that there is at present no element specifically dealing with Church schools in the National Professional Qualification for Headship, and we invite the Church of England Board of Education to raise this matter with the College.

**6.19** The Church colleges of higher education are the natural partners of the Church in this task of developing leaders, and teachers should be able to look to them for opportunities to learn about issues specific to Church schools. The development of the Church Colleges' Certificates on a national basis and their availability by distance learning are necessary so that the need can be met. (We refer to this further in paragraphs 6.29–6.31 and 9.27.) We welcome the contributions that Church schools are already making to the supply of teachers through the provision of opportunities for teaching practice and in contributing to school-based training initiatives such as the Graduate Teacher Programme. We would also welcome the more widespread application and development of schemes such as the Diocese of York's Archbishop's Training Certificate for Church of England School Teachers, preferably with some form of national accreditation.

**6.20** As an important signal to the inclusiveness of the Church's mission to the nation and of the high value it places on teachers from ethnic minorities, **we recommend that the Church should find new ways of encouraging the recruitment of teachers from minority ethnic groups.** There is also a concern that the proportion of men teaching in primary schools is very small. Ways of encouraging more men into the profession need to be found.

### (c) Help for primary heads in small schools

**6.21** The 1990s were characterized by increasingly heavy administrative demands on teachers and headteachers as Governments introduced successive initiatives in the pursuit of high standards of achievement. **We advocate now a period of greater stability** so that the benefits of all these initiatives can be realized, with teachers needing to commit less time to planning for, and administering, change, to the benefit of the energies they can devote to teaching. Even so, in a rapidly changing world schools will never be free from change. In view of the sustained pressures on schools to achieve, the extensive consultations in which we have engaged have given us a particular concern about the heads of small primary schools which are typical of village communities and whose well-being matters very much to the character and identity of the whole community.

**6.22** The Church has a particularly large number of small and very small primary schools, in which the head spends at least three or four days teaching. In addition, many primary school heads often have to go into classes to relieve curriculum coordinators or to cover staff absences. In rural schools, Church school heads are an important part of the Church's supporting ministry for their surrounding communities, where there can often be a high degree of rural deprivation. But small schools are to be found in other areas too. The burden on these heads of running the school and at the same time coping with the flow of statutory requirements and initiatives, however desirable they are, can be overwhelming. This strain is reflected in the level of long-term sickness, early retirements and the small number of good candidates for headships. The successful teaching of the full National Curriculum and RE and ministering to children and parents are challenge enough and the heads of such schools need help or relief. In spite of these pressures, it is worth noting, however, that in terms of SATs results small schools are often highly successful.

**6.23** It has been put to us that governing bodies should be vigilant to see that their heads in these small schools do not exhaust themselves by taking a greater teaching load than they should, and also to see that they take proper opportunities for professional development. We agree. For these and other heads, a sabbatical break during their term as a head could be an opportunity to gain refreshment, new ideas and a renewed commitment to the task.

**6.24** **We would strongly recommend that the Church at national level should see it as one of its prime responsibilities to work with the Government to achieve a reduction in the personal administrative load on the heads of small primary schools to a realistic level.** We recognize that government has already provided some welcome additional funding to help small schools with their administration, but more needs to be done. It may be that a study should be mounted with Government and other interested parties to see how that can best be achieved. The analogy of the way Government has acted in the industrial sector to reduce the legislative and administrative burden on small firms may be relevant. There may be opportunities for developing 'cluster' arrangements for small schools, offering support through curriculum leaders and others, or for greater use of 'pyramid' structures in which secondary schools can play a part in helping small primary schools. **The Church should establish, in partnership with the DfEE and other interested bodies, a 'small schools unit' to foster best practice across the country.**

## The wider issue

**6.25** The issues facing the Church go well beyond the three actions we have identified as especially urgent, in improving teacher morale, in fostering respect for teachers, in developing new headteachers and other leaders, and in helping the headteachers of small schools. Although some dioceses report no difficulty in filling vacancies with good teachers who are also practising Christians, that is not the general experience. We have often heard of the dilemma facing governors and headteachers, in seeking to appoint the best teacher, of the choice between candidates who are practising Christians and those who are not. Unless action is taken by the Church to encourage Christians to see teaching as a valued profession and to show by its actions how it values its Christian teachers, both within and outside Church schools, the long-term prospect is daunting.

**6.26** One diocese said in its evidence:

> 'The Church needs to promote teaching as a vocation of equal status to the priesthood.'

We agree. We would add that vocation does not imply that teaching should be regarded as a profession that does not need to be appropriately remunerated. Indeed it must be if the nation is to get the quality of education our children need. We include as Appendix 5 to the report a brief memorandum by the Archbishop of Wales on Christian vocation. By a Christian vocation we mean not just a judgement by a Christian that teaching is 'what I want to do'. We mean a realization that it is a ministry in, of, and to the body of Christ. For a Christian, a vocation to teach should be the context in which he or she understands himself or herself called to act and speak for God. In that sense, it is something wonderful that stands alongside a vocation to the priesthood. Although Christian teachers are vital for Church schools they are also of immense value in Community schools and Special schools. **We would therefore recommend that through the dioceses all parishes should be urged, not just once but repeatedly, to put before people what it means to be a Christian teacher and in appropriate cases encourage a vocation to teach.**

**6.27** Parishes could, for example, provide opportunities for people to develop their teaching skills through voluntary work. Parish-based children's work and youth groups provide a structured environment for developing their skills in planning and in teaching children. In encouraging the vocation to teach, parishes should know that dioceses can offer them information that will be helpful to those who are interested in becoming Christian teachers about equipping themselves to enter the profession. The Church colleges of higher education should come to mind as the kinds of institutions where Christians can look for a learning environment where it is comfortable to be a Christian and where the Christian faith is fostered. **We therefore invite parishes and dioceses to establish appropriate relationships and communication with the Church colleges.**

**6.28** Turning to those in the profession, and the concern to retain teachers in the profession, as we have said in an earlier part of this chapter it matters very much that the Church should show through its actions that the vocation to teach by Christians is highly valued and respected. We have noted the emphasis placed by a number of bishops we have met on demonstrating this in their programmes of visiting and in the close knowledge they have of schools in the diocese. **Every bit as important is the support of the bishops and parishes for Christian teachers who are giving valued service in Community schools and Special schools** where the confession of the faith may be difficult and where they may encounter hostility from some.

**6.29** One way of providing enhanced opportunities for Christians seeking Qualified Teacher Status (QTS) has been to offer specific additional qualifications designed to meet the needs of new entrants to work in Church schools. The Catholic Certificate in Religious Studies (CCRS) and its recent variations have provided a well-established route for teachers entering Roman Catholic schools. The energy invested in the Certificate over the years by Roman Catholic schools and dioceses has meant that it is now a well-established requirement for many teachers working in that sector. Some colleges now offer the certificate as an option within a programme leading to Qualified Teacher Status (QTS). The Church of England largely abandoned its provision of specialist courses at this level during the 1960s and 1970s, and it was only in the late 1980s that any attempts were made to re-establish the position. The creation of the Church Colleges' Certificate in Church School Studies has provided the potential to re-establish a basic qualification for teaching in Anglican schools. At the current time, a number of Anglican colleges offer this Certificate to their students and to teachers or governors working in Church schools. It would clearly be desirable for all new or recently qualified teachers in Anglican schools to hold this Certificate as part of their professional preparation for work in a Church school. We are a long way from achieving that goal.

**6.30** We have noted the success of the CCRS and its popularity. Roman Catholic schools always require teachers who are seeking promotion within a school to hold the Catholic Certificate.

**6.31** **We invite the Anglican Church colleges to continue working together to develop the Church Colleges' Certificate in Church School Studies or Religious Studies and the award of credits towards professional qualifications.** It may well be that some of the substance of the CCRS would be relevant to the Anglican Certificate in Religious Studies. A master's degree in Church School Education has been developed and is currently available from five of the Church colleges, either as a taught course or by distance learning (or a combination of the two).

**6.32** We have referred in Chapter 4 to the importance of high quality religious education in Church schools. Taking the whole community of schools, we have been concerned to read a comment that for as long as OFSTED has been keeping records of school inspection reports, RE has been one of the subjects in which pupils' learning is weakest. We have heard that there are particular problems at Key Stage 3. The quality of learning in any subject depends to a large extent on the support it is given by the headteacher and the recognition given to subject teachers. **We would therefore invite the Church to work for the greater recognition and status of RE teachers in all schools by the provision of an appropriate career structure and corresponding salary scales and resources, and to support them in responding to the demands placed upon them and in fostering the take-up of at least the GCSE short course in religious studies which helps to give a focus and commitment to the subject at Key Stage 4.**

**6.33** We have received many other suggestions for practical action which we would commend to the Church, and drawing upon these and the discussion above we list examples of these in our detailed recommendations shown below. In offering them, **we repeat that the need for sustained action by the whole Church in encouraging and supporting the teachers we have, and promoting the vocation to teach, is the most important issue facing us if** our schools are to be able to take the opportunities that are now apparent and which are a great encouragement in an age where the active practice of the faith through Church membership is less committed than in previous generations.

These recommendations are as follows:

- Christian teachers should encourage suitable pupils to think of teaching as a vocation and if it seems right for the pupils encourage them to think of going to a Church college for their higher education and their teaching qualification.

- Church schools should encourage pupils to take the GCSE in RE (see also 4.13).

- The Church Colleges' Certificates in Church School Studies and in Religious Studies should be made available by the colleges on a national basis, both through college courses and distance learning, and dioceses should actively encourage the take up of these qualifications by practising teachers as well as by entrants to the profession.

- Archbishops and bishops should affirm Christian teachers by pastoral visits to schools and through inviting Christian teachers in Church and Community schools, including Special schools, to appropriate events. Dioceses should work towards greater involvement in supporting associations of Christian teachers.

- Dioceses should show the importance the Church attributes to the appointment of headteachers by a Service of Commissioning of the kind that has been agreed in some dioceses.

- Education Sunday should be celebrated in all parishes and the service should actively involve Christian teachers. It should be an occasion when the clergy speak on the vocation to teach and the value the Church places on the work of Christian teachers in all schools. From time to time, the celebration of Education Sunday should involve invitations to teachers from across the diocese to attend a service in the Cathedral.

- Attention should be drawn to the support structures already available through, e.g., the Association of Anglican Secondary School Headteachers, the Association of Christian Teachers and the National Society.

- It should be recognized that training schemes for teenage volunteers who help in parish-based children's groups can provide for some participants the beginning of a sense of vocation.

- Diocesan vocations advisers should encourage a vocation to teach as well as to the ordained ministry.

- Materials should be prepared which will help all those who have the opportunity to encourage people to consider teaching as a professional vocation.

- Governors should see it as a core part of their role to relate personally to all members of staff individually and to encourage parents to show they value what teachers are doing for their children.

- Church schools should make it a particular care to maintain contact with qualified teachers who have left the profession to have children or to pursue another career.

*chapter 7*
# The ministry, the Church and the parish

## Introduction

**7.1** The Church of England has some 4,700 Church schools, and most clergy will have one of these in their parish at some point in their ministry. Often the number of pupils in a Church school will outnumber the number currently counted as Sunday worshippers on any particular Sunday, and in national terms if recent trends continue, within a few years, the number in Church schools may well exceed the number of Sunday worshippers.

**7.2** Where a parish does not include a Church school, clergy who are seen to be at home and effective in a school, and who are respected by teachers for their professionalism, may well find that there is a welcome for them, and the opportunity to make a valued contribution, in a goodly number of Community schools.

**7.3** It matters therefore that clergy should be well equipped for ministry in and through schools, and this is especially so in relation to Church schools, whether they are Voluntary Aided, Voluntary Controlled, or Foundation schools. This has clear implications for the training of clergy. Although our consultation has underlined the pressures on the curriculum in theological colleges, courses and schemes, **the response to consultation has no less underlined the concern among diocesan boards of education that clergy should be equipped for their ministry in schools by a carefully thought through approach in pre- and post-ordination training.**

## Relationships between school and Church

**7.4** In the introduction (Chapter 1) we illustrated diagramatically the way in which we saw the Church schools coming into the heart of the life of the parishes. Our diagram is saying that Church schools are not 'an add-on', but integral to the life and ministry of the local church. Reciprocally, Church schools, whether Voluntary Aided or Controlled, should see themselves as a living, collaborating part of the Church community, each knowing that it is supported by the prayers and ministry of the other.

**7.5** In saying this, we put emphasis on the involvement of the whole Church community, rather than the incumbent alone. Already, and especially for clergy with several parishes, the load being carried is very heavy. And even with the involvement in education of Church members who have special gifts for work in schools, we recognize that for the clergy to minister to schools as they would wish may well require some heartsearching reordering of their priorities. It may, for example, involve some reduction in the administrative load on parishes or increased secretarial support. It may lead to the need for the further adoption of collaborative ministry teams across parishes. It may require the transfer of some functions, at least in part, to readers and other Church members. Such rethinking will be needed, to varying degrees, in all parishes, and nowhere more so than in the rural ministry, where the clergy commonly serve several parishes.

**7.6** The best balance of ministry to the Church school between the incumbent and the worshipping community must reflect the extent to which the clergy are gifted or qualified by training for work in schools. We have more to say on training later. All the clergy including those not well gifted for this work will want to demonstrate their loving care for their Church school (or schools), in counselling staff experiencing personal difficulties, in being seen often in and around the school, and in developing the framework of ongoing relationships between church and school. The incumbent will encourage the school to see that the children become familiar with the main liturgy, and reciprocally see that the ministry to the school is on the agenda for meetings of the Parochial Church Council (PCC) from time to time during the year. Education Sunday will be a special occasion for the church community, when, for example, the presence of a Church school in the parish will be celebrated, and its place in the life of the parish recognized and promoted.

**7.7** For its part the Church school should continually be asking itself how it can support the life of the Church community. It will want to provide an education in which children see the Church as a familiar and friendly place. It will encourage visits from the clergy and lay people according to their gifts and help them by constructive, caring advice on how to be effective and at home in the school.

**7.8** Church secondary schools normally have to relate to a large number of parishes. These parishes should support the link with the school, but the parish in which the school resides will be key to the development of the relationship and the comments we make above about the relationship between the parish church and primary schools apply. There will, however, need to be awareness of the diversity of practice within the parishes where pupils live, and schools should expect support from deaneries in responding to that diversity.

We make the following recommendations:

- **All parishes and all Church schools should reflect on the implications of the General Synod Resolution that Church schools are at the centre of the Church's mission in terms of their own parish and their own school, taking into account the comments above (7.4–7.8) and later in this chapter.**

- **Deaneries should be active in fostering the kind of relationship we have outlined and offer practical guidance to PCCs in developing their relationship and sharing best practice.**

- **Parishes and schools should pray regularly for each other.**

- **The clergy appointments procedure should ensure that, where there is a Church school in the parish, prospective clergy are given a job description that makes explicit their responsibilities towards that school.**

- The headteacher of the Church school should be involved in the welcome and induction of a new cleric.

- The parish church should welcome and celebrate the arrival of a new headteacher to its school.

- Whether or not the Chair of the governors of the Church school, the incumbent should always be involved in the selection of a new head and new teaching staff.

- Where it is the practice for the parish to be involved in the appointment of a new incumbent, the headteacher of the Church school in the parish should be involved.

- Deaneries and parishes should ensure that the Local Education Authority's child protection policy is in place and that appropriate training has been provided for the clergy and lay people involved in school ministry.

- Dioceses should be ready to assist clergy and school heads if the relationship between school and parish is in disrepair.

## The contribution of the clergy

**7.9** A new incumbent should discuss with a headteacher the ways in which his/her experience would best fit with the current needs of the school. The list of possibilities includes:

- pastor to staff, pupils and families
- ex-officio governor (and, if elected, Chair of governors)
- leader of collective worship
- consultant over collective worship and RE
- chaplain and (voluntary) teacher.

**7.10** We put the role of pastor first on our list, and while we see the incumbent being a member of the governing body we would counsel careful reflection and a reading of the advice of the National Society on the advantages and disadvantages of being Chair of a governing body in the particular parish/school context. Today especially, this role is an onerous and time-consuming responsibility, and one that requires specific strategic and administrative skills. On the other hand, as one diocese commented on the Consultation Report, if the incumbent is not the Chair 'there is a fear and some evidence in this diocese that an incumbent will allow other pressures to direct him/her from the mission of the Church through the medium of the school'. This suggests that if the incumbent does not take the chair at a Voluntary Aided school, a member of the PCC should accept responsibility to be a member, if not the Chair, of the governing body, and is charged to ensure that matters relating to the school feature on the agenda of the PCC from time to time during the year.

## Chaplains

**7.11** A significant number of Church secondary schools have a chaplain and we have seen how valuable this is, even though financial considerations may mean that it is likely to be for a limited number of hours a week or combined with a teaching appointment. Our attention has been drawn to the helpful practice in some Church secondary schools of having a voluntary year group chaplain (clerical or lay) who moves up the school with the particular year group and works closely with the head of year. The National Society has, in association with chaplains, developed a model job and person specification for chaplaincy (available on its website, www.natsoc.org.uk). We commend this to schools, especially to those who have not had a chaplain and are considering the possibility of having one.

## Worship and spiritual growth

**7.12** Church schools, through their understanding of the importance and centrality of worship, create imaginative approaches which can contribute powerfully to the spiritual development of their pupils. Many schools and churches provide human and other resources to engage pupils' interest and encourage them to think and reflect. Churches, in their own worship, should be sensitive to the various styles of worship provided by the schools and provide opportunities for the worshipping life of the school to be shared within the body of the Church congregation. One diocese, in its comments, said:

> 'One of the most essential aspects of the link between Church and school is to establish transferable patterns of worship. We are very concerned that collective worship in schools . . . does [not] have any common features or transferability to the worship in churches on Sunday.'

This is perhaps as much a comment on practice in churches as practice in schools, and it suggests a needs for reflection on both sides. However that may be, it helps immensely if a Church school in a parish is caught up in the whole life of the parish and the worshipping community engages actively with the school. Church and school should work together to bring life, colour, vigour and rigour to the gospel.

**7.13** Church schools have the capacity to create an atmosphere in which God can be discussed naturally and without apology. This will include worship in which young people are given opportunity to be aware of the transcendent and respond in a personal way that is in keeping with their culture and is relevant to their experience. In a mixed faith setting, the Church school can develop inclusive ways of expressing the Anglican tradition in collective worship.

**7.14** Practice in relation to the Eucharist varies widely in Church schools, as does the practice of parishes in admitting young people to receive the sacrament. The celebration of the Eucharist is more common in Aided than in Controlled schools, but overall the Eucharist is celebrated in about half of the Church schools. Its increasing practice means that a growing number of headteachers and clergy are advocating that pupils should not only be taught about the Eucharist in RE, but should experience what it is like to take part and share in the atmosphere of this central Christian rite. They are reflecting the view expressed in one of the National Society's former publications (*Clergy and Church Schools* by Janina Ainsworth) that 'children in Church schools, like anyone else linked to the household of faith, should have access to the special way of relating to God and Jesus provided by the Eucharist'.

**7.15** While we counsel that the celebration of the Eucharist should be encouraged in Church schools, the diversity of our schools, local Church tradition and the careful way in which parishes and dioceses are implementing the House of Bishops' Guidelines on the Admission of Baptized Persons to Holy Communion before Confirmation, makes it inappropriate to propose a policy that would be right for all. **As a preliminary to decisions made in this significant area we would emphasize the importance of extensive and sensitive consultation with all relevant parties.** Help and advice should be sought from diocesan schools and children's advisers.

## The training of the clergy

**7.16** The responses to our thoughts on the training of clergy in the Consultation Report showed a division of view between some commenting from the standpoint of the theological colleges, course and schemes and those commenting on behalf of diocesan boards of education.

**7.17** The relevant section of our Consultation Report read as follows:

> *We begin with a quotation from the evidence put to the Committee by the Church of England Board of Education and the National Society:*
>
> 'It would be quite wrong for the Board and the Society not to reflect in its submission of evidence the frustration that is felt in both diocesan and national Board of Education teams about the lack of priority given to training ordinands and inexperienced clergy in relation to Church schools and work with children and young people in general.'
>
> This is a concern expressed to us many times during the course of our work. If our Church schools are at the heart of the Church's mission to the nation, then ministerial training must equip clergy for ministry in schools. Links with schools cannot be regarded as an 'extra', but as integral to the life and ministry of the Church. In reflecting a view widely put to us in our consultations we have in mind, as noted in the opening paragraph of this chapter, that the number of pupils in Church schools is often comparable with the number of worshippers currently counted on any given Sunday.
>
> We readily acknowledge the difficulties and the already crowded curriculum of the theological colleges, course and schemes. We note that practice among these varies and that the practice of some suggests that there is scope for change. We ask the Church to accept that this training is a major need, and we invite comments on how that need can

> best be met. It is one of a small number of issues that we would put at the heart of the action that we recommend should follow the completion of our work. Among the issues on which we would welcome comment under this heading are:
>
> - what role the Church colleges might best play in contributing to pre- and post-ordination training.
> - whether there is need to strengthen the practical as opposed to the theoretical side of this preparation and if so how.
> - to what extent web-based programmes of distance learning would be an aid to post ordination development and if so how could that be integrated with practical experience.

**7.18** The principal of one of the courses commented:

> 'Your report nods toward the problem of the crowded curriculum – it is impossibly crowded precisely because of a plethora of recommendations over the years on all manner of topics. I believe that for a working party to come up with recommendations of such specificity misunderstands the nature of ordination training and the nature of the pastoral problem about ministry in Church schools.'

whilst the principal of a scheme (for ordained local ministers) wrote:

> 'the amount of time available for highlighting specific ministries, such as ministry in schools, pastoring the family of suicides, leading Bible-study groups, preaching on Remembrance Sunday, and the host of other ministries is limited.'

**7.19** The alternative view is reflected in the following two quotations from diocesan boards of education:

> 'How can Church schools be at the centre of the Church's mission to the nation if this is not recognized in initial ministerial training?'
>
> and
>
> 'All newly ordained clergy should leave college with the theology of education at the heart of the parish mission and some skills to overcome their fear of school worship.'

**7.20** We do wish to recognize that the curriculum of the colleges, courses and schemes is indeed crowded, that they have been subjected to pressure to include various special aspects of ministry, and that there is a limit to what they can cover. We no less accept that the fundamentals that apply to the understanding of ministry must govern the curriculum. It is not for us to judge what is important and what is not quite so important, and what therefore must be left to post-ordination training. But recognizing the limits we invite consideration that initial ministerial education should offer ordinands:

- a basic understanding of the ecclesiology and missiology of Church schools and their legal basis;
- wherever possible, brief placements – arranged during the school term – during pre-ordination training in a parish with a Church school or failing that in a parish with a Community school where the incumbent is engaged;
- where the pre-ordination programme covers two or more academic years a module on Church schools, where this can reasonably be offered as an option to supplement the basic curriculum.

**7.21** The main focus of training will, however, have to be after ordination. Accordingly, the focus of post-ordination training in relation to schools must be strongly developed. It needs to be structured by the dioceses and should sensibly involve the Church colleges of higher education, which have the necessary expertise in teaching and schools. We would also suggest that where possible a curate's first appointment should be to a parish with a Church school or a Community school where the incumbent is active.

**7.22** We are also conscious that the educational world is continually developing and that the post-ordination training will need updating from time to time. We are no less conscious that some clergy might wish to benefit from an enhancement of their skills in ministering to schools. The dioceses will need to consider how this can best be offered, especially when an incumbent moves into a parish with a Church school. We would add that the Web offers an increasingly valuable source of support for clergy, who can access it from the parish office, or local school or library. For example, the National Society (www.natsoc.org.uk) and the Society for Promoting Christian Knowledge (www.assemblies.org.uk) both seek to offer, to quote one of them, 'high quality, lively primary assemblies at the touch of a button'.

**7.23** We conclude this section therefore with a recommendation that a small expert group should be established to provide advice to dioceses on a structured approach to the post-ordination training of clergy in developing their effectiveness in schools, and in helping established clergy to enhance their skills in schools, as needed, throughout their careers. The group should include a Church college of higher education in its membership. Such help should encompass access to high quality web-based material.

*chapter 8*
# Leadership, management and governance

## The headteacher

**8.1** Church school headteachers are spiritual and academic leaders of the school. Excellence in headship requires visionary, inspired leadership and management centred on the school as a worshipping community, where educational and academic excellence for all pupils is pursued in a Christian context. Although not formally recognized as such by the Church, it is arguable that since Church school headship involves religious and spiritual leadership, to the Christian it comprises a form of lay ministry, which is complementary to the Church's ordained ministry.

**8.2** It is the creation of a distinctive Christian community that marks out the role of a headteacher in a Church school. It is a particularly challenging and demanding role, and its purpose cannot be achieved by command. It is rather something that has to be achieved by the headteacher living the values that she or he seeks to establish and winning a willing acceptance of those values by staff in particular, but also by children and parents, all of whom, even though it may not be explicitly recognized, will relate individually to the headteacher.

**8.3** There is no one right model of leadership. Headteachers need to respond to time and circumstance, capitalizing on their inherent strengths and seeking support from colleagues in their areas of weakness. Each will develop a distinctive style. In view of the special dimension of leadership in a Church school identified in the preceding paragraph, we think it may be helpful to offer an insight into elements within this distinctive leadership which has been suggested to us during our work.

**8.4** This suggestion is that one possible approach to understanding the headteacher's leadership role is to see it as encompassing three main aspects. Firstly, the headteacher can be viewed as a *servant*-leader, working to encourage the educational and spiritual growth of pupils. Secondly, the headteacher has a pre-eminent role in setting the overall tone of the school, and in ensuring that Christian values permeate the whole life of the school. This role could be described as *transformational* leadership, in that the headteacher will take the lead in nurturing the development of a Christian community, encouraging its spiritual growth and awareness and offering a clear and recognizable sense of Christian purpose. Thirdly, the headteacher will provide *invitational* leadership, welcoming all into the school, offering reassurance and affirmation, recognizing the value of individuals, and inviting the school community to share the good news of the kingdom. We do not offer these insights in a prescriptive sense, but as a basis for reflection by those preparing for, or reviewing, their own personal approach to leadership.

**8.5** Headteachers need support in their roles, both through prayer and in practical terms. We know that the short induction programmes offered by some dioceses for new headteachers are very much appreciated by them. **We would suggest that where it is not already the practice to do so, dioceses should arrange for new headteachers to come together to review their experiences after, say, three months, and that if they wish it an experienced headteacher is asked to be a guide, counsellor and friend for the first year. There may be occasions when these mentoring arrangements can be worked out on an ecumenical basis.** At the secondary level, the Association of Anglican Secondary School Headteachers provides a valuable forum for fellowship and the sharing of experience and good practice. One diocese in its comments has advocated the creation of a parallel organization for primary school heads.

## Governors

**8.6** We have stressed in Chapter 6 the key role of the governing body in developing respect for teachers and securing support for them from parents. A strong, well-led governing body, supportive of the school, its teachers and its mission makes an important contribution to the school's well-being and effectiveness. The foundation governors will have an especial care for the school's Christian character. With the increased devolution of responsibilities from local education authorities to governing bodies, governors' duties are onerous. There has been much public comment on the need to reduce the administrative burden on teachers. It applies with equal force to governors and was the source of comment in the responses to consultation. We therefore welcome the measures government has announced to cut back the flow of paper to schools. It is fundamental to good governance and to the willingness of busy people to accept the responsibilities of governorship. **Cutting back the flow of paper into schools is a matter which we recommend the Church of England Board of Education should keep on its agenda in its dealings with Government on behalf of governors and teachers, as relevant both to the effectiveness of schools, as well as to the recruitment, retention and motivation of teachers and governors.**

**8.7** In governing bodies this applies in particular to the Chairs for whom the time commitment is particularly demanding. We have commented in paragraph 7.10 on the issue of whether the incumbent should take the chair. The time commitment must be a factor in the decision, and may be a compelling one where the incumbent serves several parishes with schools. This is especially relevant in rural areas.

**8.8** For those coming into school governorship some short, practical training through the diocese is a great help and we note that this is the practice in a number of dioceses. With the busy lives people lead this will be as much as is possible for most governors. But for some, and we hope an increasing number, a more formal programme to develop skills and knowledge will be welcome, leading to formal recognition. This may come from a National Vocational Qualification, but there have been recent moves to create a version of the Church Colleges' Certificate in Church Schools for Church school governors providing a well-structured course of training which goes beyond immediate utility. It is a useful response to those willing to commit time and energy to train as a governor that this should be recognized by an award that has value in academic and employment terms. Set at this academic level, for some it could serve as an access course to higher education. For those at a distance from a college, the provision of material through distance learning, including web-based modules, could be particularly helpful. We believe that in collaboration with LEAs etc., **dioceses should encourage and facilitate practical training for governors, and for foundation governors in particular, and encourage the taking up of the Church Colleges Certificates by those seeking a high level of training, carrying with it formal recognition.**

**8.9** When there is difficulty in filling governors' places, especially from **candidates with a Christian commitment, we suggest seeking candidates from elsewhere in the diocese, at least on a temporary basis.** This strategy would not only assist in safeguarding the nature of the foundation of the school, but would also widen the sphere of participation across the diocese, creating a greater sense of involvement and ownership.

**8.10** The prime personal responsibility of the Chair is the effective conduct of business by the governing body. **We recommend therefore that the Chair is amongst those always consulted by dioceses about filling vacancies so that the needs of the governing body in terms of skills balance, values, experience and ethnicity are fully taken into account.** We understand that this is not the invariable practice and consultation showed that not all dioceses agree with this recommendation, arguing that the consultation should be with the incumbent, the PCC and foundation governors, or that consultation with the Chair may be inappropriate. We are not arguing, however, that the Chair's view should carry the day, but that the Chair should be amongst those consulted.

## The role of Diocesan Boards of Education (DBEs)

**8.11** The functions of DBEs are stated in the Diocesan Boards of Education Measure 1991 and are to:

- promote education in the diocese, being education which is consistent with the faith and practice of the Church of England;
- promote religious education and worship in schools in the diocese;
- promote Church schools in the diocese;
- advise governors and trustees on any matters affecting Church schools;
- promote cooperation between the Board and other groups and agencies concerned with education in the diocese;
- undertake functions assigned to the Board by the Diocesan Synod.

It should be noted that the Measure provides for a structural partnership between the Government and the Church through the DBEs.

**8.12** The Measure, to a great extent, gives commonality to the core work of DBEs in their involvement with schools, but the nature, range and scope of the work of individual Boards bring a measure of complexity that inhibits adoption of a single model. A survey made in 1995 by Culham College

Institute pointed to an 'increasing differentiation between schools and non-schools work, with the former operating increasingly under a different set of rules and in a different environment in terms of both market and finance'. This reflected a trend away from holding together in dioceses statutory and voluntary education work. Some Diocesan Boards regret this trend and one has stated quite strongly its view that a single Board of Education and training with responsibility for adult, youth, children and continuing ministerial education as well as schools and further education makes possible real collaboration and reciprocal insights. By retaining the traditional association between statutory and voluntary work, the Board and presumably the diocese would be helped to think of the school and parish as an organic whole. **We would encourage dioceses to reflect on the benefit to be gained from a single broad structure**, not least in the context of a society committed to the practice of life-long learning where schools have the potential to become family learning centres. As one diocese put it, 'We're powerful connected, wasted apart.'

**8.13** The work of the DBE needs to be fully integrated into the strategy of a diocese. One diocesan director of education (DDE) in evidence has warned of a danger that 'Church schools [might] become a technical enterprise that a diocese is grateful that somebody "fixes" on its behalf'. This danger could become a reality with the increasing legislative framework and its plethora of attendant codes of practice, circulars and statutory instruments requiring a greater range of technical understanding and attention by DBE officers. To counter this possibility, it is essential that the diocese recognizes this work as an integral part of an overall strategy for seeing Church schools as central to their mission. In the light of these comments, **we suggest that dioceses review their present arrangements for education and training.**

**8.14** The other essential partners of the DBEs are the local education authorities, the Church of England Board of Education and the DfEE; a point that has been reflected again and again in the evidence presented to us. There is strong recognition by DDEs of the necessity to work very closely with their local education authority colleagues and of the value they place on their professional advice, support and collaboration. Reciprocally the responses by the local educational authorities and the DfEE show how warmly the level of collaboration that has been established by dioceses is welcomed.

**8.15** The resourcing and staffing of DBEs becomes an immediate issue if our recommendations on the expansion of provision are to be successfully implemented. A major increase in provision will have a commensurate increase in the level of work generated and the technical expertise needed to carry it out effectively. The financing of the work of DBEs is complex, possibly requiring a separate piece of research, but evidence, both written and verbal, from a number of sources, including headteachers, calls for more resourcing of DBEs in order to maintain and strengthen further their quota of staff that will be credible, experienced and professional. This is particularly relevant when an expansion of school provision is taking place (see Chapter 5).

**8.16** With increased resourcing, more focused accountability may be required. The evidence received does not present a clear picture of accountability processes. However, we welcome the development of a model for this by a small group of diocesan directors of education. This is based on self-evaluation and review, enhanced by external evaluation. Some argue that dioceses are too disparate a group for a common review model for use across all dioceses. However, using the framework of the Diocesan Boards of Education Measure mentioned above, some areas of commonality may be identified. **We suggest that, for the purposes of credibility and authority, such a model for accountability could be used nationally, with modification where necessary, and put into practice in consultation with National Society/Church of England Board of Education officers. This is a matter we invite dioceses to consider when they next review their arrangements.** In making this suggestion we would emphasize that the purpose of accountability of this kind is to assist hard-working people to stand back from day to day pressures and make a dispassionate assessment of their own stewardship, with external evaluation offering encouragement and insights as well as identifying areas for potential improvement.

**8.17** To obtain the best use of scarce resources **the sharing of specialist and technical expertise by DBE officers on an inter-diocesan level has also been suggested in Chapter 5, possibly on a regional basis**, and possibly, as appropriate, extending to Roman Catholic dioceses. We illustrate how this might be realized for the proposed expansion of secondary provision incorporating the consequent expertise needed for such an enterprise in paragraph 5.27. It could also be a vehicle through which the collaborating dioceses support a diocese with a school in difficulty. Regional teams could provide the initial pool of technical support needed by diocesan directors of education (DDEs) as appropriate to their circumstances. In turn, the respective DDEs will have the essential local knowledge and credibility at both diocesan and local education authority level. We believe that the synergy created by such combined forces may well provide a model for future work in other areas of the DBEs' range of responsibilities. **We recommend the creation of such capabilities by groups of dioceses.** But we add, it is important that any such capability, and especially a regional task force, works through and in support of the dioceses concerned: it must in no way become an alternative source of support and advice to the diocese.

*chapter 9*
# The Church colleges

## Introduction

**9.1** The Church colleges of higher education have a central place in our thinking as natural places in a changing world to which the Church should look for developing Christian teachers and for providing their continuing professional development for leadership roles. They also have a central role to play in ensuring a strong Christian presence in education at all levels and in all sectors. This leads us to be concerned that the Church colleges should be secure in their distinctively Christian character; and that their continued existence into the long term can be ensured.

## The colleges

**9.2** There are eleven higher education colleges in England and one in Wales with an Anglican foundation. Of these, nine are free standing Anglican institutions; three involve partnerships. All are part of a wider grouping of colleges in England and Wales known as the Council of Church Colleges (CCC). Further details of the colleges are given in Appendix 4.

**9.3** Ten of the colleges were founded in the nineteenth century as part of a move to raise standards in Church elementary schools for the children of the poor through effective arrangements for training teachers. Teacher training was also the major founding purpose of the two colleges created in the 1960s.

**9.4** The fortunes of the colleges have been closely affected by changes in national policy for teacher training. For example, the major national reduction in teacher training in the 1970s and early 1980s was the main reason for the reduction in the number of Anglican colleges from 27 in 1970 to 12 in 1982. Changes to the arrangements for the inspection and funding of teacher training since 1997 have led to a further round of closures and mergers of higher education colleges but the Anglican colleges which have performed very well in inspection have not so far been affected.

**9.5** Although the number of Anglican higher education colleges has decreased since 1970, the overall size of Anglican higher education has increased greatly over the same period. Thus when there were 27 colleges the peak number of students was about 19,000; now there are nearly 64,000. On the other hand, with cut backs in national programmes for the training of teachers the number of full-time students in Initial Teacher Training (ITT) in Church colleges has fallen from a peak of 19,000 to the 12,000 today (see Appendix 4). But the share of the national total of ITT places enjoyed by the Church colleges has risen from about a sixth to a quarter. It will be immediately apparent that there is a large number of other higher education institutions providing ITT, and many Christians choose to attend these institutions outside the Church colleges sector. The provision for these lies outside our terms of reference, but we are aware of the welcome presence of chaplains to support them and that many teachers in Church schools look back with gratitude to their experience in those colleges and universities.

**9.6** To return to the Church colleges as a group, teacher education makes up more than a quarter of their total activity. All 12 colleges are involved in teacher training and in two colleges (St Mark and St John, and Bishop Grosseteste) teacher training accounts for more than 50 per cent of the activity. Nearly one third of all students in England training to be primary teachers and about 15 per cent of those training to be secondary teachers are in the Anglican colleges, and the colleges currently produce about 33 per cent of primary and about 17 per cent of secondary teachers in England. The colleges are also major providers of continuing professional development courses for teachers, with St Mark and St John the second and St Martin's the third largest providers in England.

**9.7** The Church colleges have, however, become much more broadly based and much larger than the teacher training institutions created in the past. They are major providers of healthcare education and other important areas of provision include the social sciences, art and design, business and administration, and the humanities.

**9.8** The comparative quality of the Church colleges is high. Inspection grades for teacher training courses are well above the national averages, as are course completion rates, especially when account is taken of the percentages of mature students in the colleges.

**9.9** In many ways, the colleges are diverse. They vary considerably in size (from 1,000 to more than 10,000 students) and in the scope of their work. They also vary with regard to degree awarding powers and institutional title. Two institutions have degree awarding powers for both research and taught degrees and another two have degree awarding powers for taught programmes, which increases their operational flexibility and enables them to use the title University College. The remaining eight colleges prepare students for the degrees of local universities, under accreditation and/or validation arrangements.

**9.10** In spite of this diversity, the colleges share characteristics that relate in various ways to their common foundation as Anglican colleges of higher education.

**9.11** The Anglican foundation of the colleges is reflected in the arrangements for governance which involve a church body as trustee. At least one quarter and usually more than one half of the governors are appointed by a church body or bodies. The Articles of Government usually require the principal of the college to be a practising communicant member and the chaplain to be a priest in holy orders of the Anglican Church. The holders of other designated posts such as deputy principal may also be required to be practising communicant members of the Anglican Church.

**9.12** The mission statements all refer to the Christian foundation and purposes of the colleges, including the provision of opportunities for service, worship and the serious study of Christianity.

**9.13** The curriculum provided by the colleges includes many common elements which are derived from or relate directly to their Christian foundation and mission. The colleges provide 25 per cent of the places in England for secondary religious education and are substantial providers of specialist religious studies within primary initial teacher training. A number of colleges have resource centres for religious education. Nine out of the twelve colleges offer degree courses in theology and all contribute to Church education through the Church Colleges' Certificate and other programmes. The colleges have also all shared in an 'Engaging the Curriculum' project which has aimed to make available insights from Christian faith and thought to subjects offered in the colleges.

**9.14** The colleges share an aim to be supportive and welcoming communities based on Christian principles and exemplifying Christian values. Their chaplaincies and chapels ensure that worshipping Christian communities lie at the heart of the colleges. Although the colleges are inclusive communities, welcoming members of all faiths and of none, they are Christian institutions which offer a Christian influence to all staff and students.

**9.15** The colleges respond in a number of ways to the needs of the Church. They provide opportunities for Christian students, make available their resources to Church groups, provide education for members of the Church and educate teachers for Church schools. They contribute to lay and reader training and in some cases also to training for the ordained ministry. The colleges have significant links with different dioceses of the Church of England. In some cases, these links have been recently reviewed and strengthened but we find that the strength of the relationships is variable even between a diocese and a college within its see. Most dioceses do not have a college and the relationships are not well developed. **We therefore recommend action now to identify best practice as a basis for developing the relationships between colleges and all dioceses, whether they have a college or not. This is a task that might quickly be discharged by a small working group.**

**9.16** The colleges work together in partnerships in a number of important mission-related areas. They share in the Church colleges' academic programmes which coordinate work at certificate and at masters level in religious studies and in Church school education. Five of the colleges are partners in the Urban Learning Foundation, which is based in Tower Hamlets in East London and which provides opportunities, especially in teacher training, for students of the colleges, and responds in various ways to the educational needs of the people of East London.

## The two major issues

**9.17** The Church colleges have thus come a long way from their origins as institutions established as Church foundations to provide teachers in times when the Church was establishing thousands of schools. They are characteristically much larger, and most offer higher education across a broad range of subjects as well as teacher training. Their student intake is correspondingly broadly based, with practising Christians probably in a minority.

**9.18** Thus while the colleges have remained Church foundations, and have taken various measures to remain true to their foundation, the great challenge is to sustain and develop their Christian distinctiveness. From the point of view of their contribution to the Church's mission to the nation, through the Church schools, that need applies particularly to the teacher training departments. That is the first challenge to the colleges.

**9.19** The second major challenge is to continue in being for the long-term as Christian institutions. At this time, the colleges are in good financial health and have a good record for quality. However, as history shows, the colleges can be vulnerable to changing circumstances. Areas of risk include the competition with other providers to recruit students, and history points to a vulnerability reflecting the risk of major changes in the number of places which the state decides to fund in teacher training. Also in teacher training, the identification of poor performance through inspection can have serious adverse effects, including rapid reductions in student numbers and related funding. Although the Anglican colleges have done well in inspections of their work in teacher training, the risk relating to quality cannot ever be eliminated.

**9.20** Another factor which potentially increases the risk to the long-term stability of individual colleges lies in not having degree-awarding powers, a situation which restricts operational flexibility and which by precluding the use of university college title may also have an adverse effect on recruitment. **We recommend to the eight colleges which do not currently have degree awarding powers that they should seek such powers (either individually or through academic association) and support one another in the relevant applications.**

## The distinctiveness of Anglican colleges

**9.21** An Anglican college of higher education will have characteristics which are additional to or accorded greater importance than those found in secular institutions. Such characteristics and activities will arise from the Christian foundation and motivation of the colleges and will involve some combination of education in a Christian manner, education about Christianity and education into Christianity.

**9.22** Individual autonomous institutions are likely to act in ways which will produce differences in their detailed characteristics and activities but the response of all the institutions might be expected to be within a common framework. Such a framework might reasonably embrace all matters relating to the provision, context, purposes and stakeholders of the colleges. **A suggested framework is set out as an annex to this chapter.**

**9.23** The ways in which teachers are educated are important. The Church colleges provide a setting in which all student teachers can be informed about Church schools and given the opportunity, partly through relevant teaching practice, to prepare for careers in Church schools. The Church colleges might also be expected to meet at the highest possible quality the statutory requirements relating to religious education, spiritual and moral development and collective worship. On this basis, all Church college Newly Qualified Teachers (NQTs) whether professing Christians or not would be able to contribute effectively to relevant areas in schools. The current policy framework for teacher education, however, makes the full achievement of these objectives difficult. For example, the current circular (DfEE 4/98) setting out the requirements for teacher training courses pays relatively little attention to the relevant matters and is now seriously out of line with the new National Curriculum for schools with its emphasis on values, virtues and purposes. The continuing shift towards postgraduate provision in Initial Teacher Training (ITT), now accelerated by the introduction of training salaries for postgraduate but not for undergraduate ITT courses, reduces the opportunity to deal effectively with the matters of particular importance in Christian education mentioned above. It also reduces greatly the overall influence of the Church college experience on those training to be teachers. There may also be other losses, as research from the USA suggests that those preparing to be teachers through undergraduate programmes tend to be more committed to teaching and to stay longer in the profession.

**9.24** Faced with these changes, the colleges need to consider not only introducing new patterns of ITT but also strengthening their Continuing Professional Development (CPD) programmes in relevant areas. The objective of strengthening the Church's role in education has, in any case, major implications for professional development. Development programmes are needed not only for teachers, headteachers and those preparing to apply for headships but also for governors and for lay and ordained members of faith communities who wish to affirm and support the work of Church schools. We deal with issues relating to leadership, management and governance in Chapter 8. It is important to say here that the colleges already have substantial provision in relevant areas of CPD and that the material produced in connection with the Church Colleges' Certificate and especially for the MA programmes in Church School Studies (including the three volumes in the Religion in Education series) provides information relevant to the needs of any of the groups interested in contributing to the work of Church schools. In some cases, however, this material would need to be supplemented by provision relating specifically to the leadership and management of Church schools. The present national arrangements for training in these important areas are the responsibility of the DfEE and the TTA and are not always well matched to the particular and distinctive needs of Church schools.

**9.25** Our consultation indicated support from the Church colleges for the objective of securing and enhancing their distinctiveness and the idea of a common framework relating to distinctiveness was also generally supported. We have considered fully the comments from individual colleges and from the Council of Anglican Principals and we recognize that there will be differences in the detailed responses that individual autonomous institutions will make to **our recommendations which are as follows:**

- the colleges, individually and collectively, should take steps to secure and enhance their distinctiveness;

- the responsibility for this within individual colleges should be made clear through a formally established structure, perhaps through the creation of a Foundation Committee composed of members of the governing body and staff of the college;

- the work on distinctiveness should take account of the suggested common framework set out in the annex to this chapter.

In order to encourage and share best practice in supporting the Christian foundation of the colleges and to promote effective relationships between the colleges and the Church, **we also recommend that:**

- **a system of regular visitations to the colleges be established; these visitations would take place at intervals of, say, four or five years and would involve senior people drawn from the Church and from Church colleges other than the one being visited.**

**9.26** In seeking to secure and to enhance their distinctiveness, it is clearly helpful for the colleges to have a significant core of academic staff who are practising Christians and given the colleges' role in developing Christian teachers, this is particularly the case for their teacher training departments. We consider it essential that all those appointed to senior positions in the colleges should be in sympathy with and willing and able to support the mission of the colleges as Christian institutions. With regard to the head of teacher training, we agree with the views of the colleges that she or he should be not only of excellent academic quality but also sensitive to the Christian tradition in education and supportive of Church schools and mindful of their needs. Indeed, **we would go further and so we recommend to the colleges that as a long-term policy, the head of teacher training should be a practising Christian.**

**9.27** As described elsewhere, the Church colleges already make substantial contributions to meeting the needs of Church schools. The needs identified in this report are, however, substantial and extend not just to student teachers but also to qualified teachers (6.29– 6.31), headteachers and potential headteachers, professionally qualified diocesan staff, governors (8.8), clergy and classroom assistants. Although the Church Colleges' Certificate and masters programmes provide a good basis for meeting most of those needs, substantial further development is needed if the needs are to be met more fully. Such development should be within a framework, the elements of which would include a modular structure, a credit accumulation and transfer system, funding within standard HEFCE and TTA arrangements and qualifications at levels within the new national framework appropriate to the relevant student groups. In addition, the courses for qualified teachers, heads and potential heads should be compatible with the national arrangements for continuing professional development and for school leadership and management. **We recommend to the Church colleges that the Church college programmes are developed along the lines indicated; given the urgency of the needs and the patchy uptake of the present Church college programmes, this development might best be undertaken by a lead institution or institutions, rather than through a partnership of all the Church colleges.**

### The importance of chaplaincy

**9.28** Chaplaincy is about a concern for the whole corporate life of the institution. It includes a pastoral concern for all members of the institution and for the intellectual and spiritual growth of Christian and other students and staff. More widely, it rightly has a concern for the health of the institution itself: its vision, structures and activities.

**9.29** In essence, chaplaincy has at its centre the question of how people and their organizational structures reflect God's purpose for humanity – the realizing in human beings of the image of God through the gift of Christ's Spirit, in the conviction that the gospel shows us an understanding of that fullness of life revealed in the ministry, death and resurrection of Jesus.

**9.30** Chaplaincy has an important place in a Church college at every level: in respect of College governance, in reviewing the health of the whole institution and its structures; and in dialogue with scholars, as they grapple with academic and ethical questions to which there may not be an immediately obvious Christian dimension.

**9.31** We have been impressed by the way colleges, with whom we have discussed the role of the chaplaincy, seek to integrate the Chaplain(cy) into the decision-making processes of the institution, and we commend this practice.

## The long-term viability of the colleges

**9.32** Reference has been made (9.5) to past losses of Church colleges and to their vulnerability to sharp changes in funded student places for teacher training.

**9.33** Where, as a result of serious difficulties, a Church college has merged into a secular institution past history suggests that over time distinctiveness tends gradually to be lost. This implies that the best way of maintaining the distinctiveness of any college is through its continuation as an independent institution, and failing that, a merger with another Church college offers the best chance of preserving Christian distinctiveness.

**9.34** We therefore recommend that where the viability of a Church college becomes in doubt, the college gives early and serious consideration to a merger or other form of partnership with another Church college. We would further recommend that in view of the distinctive contribution of the Church colleges to the provision of education in schools that the Teacher Training Agency (TTA) and the Higher Education Funding Council provide appropriate transitional support to facilitate such a merger. We invite the Church at national level to pursue this matter with Government.

**9.35** Increasing and developing sensible partnerships between the Church colleges makes sense and will be most effective where the partnerships add value which is greater than the effort involved. Some writers have argued for a federation of Anglican or all Church colleges to create a federal Anglican or Christian University but these proposals have received relatively little support from the colleges, and the creation of a federal institution is not at this stage considered to be a practical proposition. Leaving aside the difficulties inherent in the stringent current framework for the approval of university title, the individual colleges are diverse and at different states of development in relation to widely different long-term aspirations. In addition, the trust deeds of most of the colleges define objects to do with the continuation of the particular institution.

**9.36** Our Consultation Report drew attention to a number of possible forms of association between institutions which would fall well short of the loss of autonomy involved in a merger. We have been encouraged by the readiness shown subsequently by members of the Council of Church Colleges to develop a more coherent expression of collective identity and a greater degree of collaboration. We note that the CCC will consider strategies for collaboration at a meeting in September 2001 and we look forward to the outcome of those deliberations.

**9.37** The long-term viability of the colleges will be enhanced if their relationships with the Church at national, diocesan and schools level are the subject of a process initiated by all partners to strengthen those relationships.

**9.38** We have recommended elsewhere (9.15) the development of a model relationship between the colleges and the dioceses and that parishes and dioceses should draw the Church colleges to the attention of Christians considering teaching as their vocation. We have also suggested (9.25) a system of regular visitations to the colleges; an important aspect of the purpose of these would be to assess the support the colleges are receiving from dioceses and parishes.

**9.39** The Church of England centrally has shown and continues to show interest in the colleges and has from time to time given general affirmation of their work (e.g. in the General Synod discussions of *An Excellent Enterprise* in 1994 and of the Church's role in education in 1998). An Advisory Group for the Church colleges has been set up recently to deal mainly with the Church's legal and financial interests in the trusteeship and governance of the colleges. It would be helpful if, in addition to these useful initiatives, the Church were to reach, in partnership with the colleges, a strategic view of the long-term purposes of the colleges in the life and work of the Church. Among other things, this strategic view might cover the role of the Church colleges in relation not only to Church schools but also to religious education and theological training including training for the ordained ministry. The Church colleges offer a tremendous potential resource to the Church. If that resource is to be fully used, the colleges need to be seen by the Church as essential and to be used as the first source of advice and support on relevant matters. Having a strategy for the colleges, backed up by appropriate supportive action would also help the Church of England to make a positive contribution to ensuring the long-term viability of its colleges.

**9.40** We recommend that the Church should develop a strategic view of its relationships with the colleges and that the Church should affirm the essential role of the colleges through using the colleges as the first source of advice on relevant matters. We also invite the Church to consider what long-term role the Church colleges might have in the pre- and post-ordination training of the clergy. The colleges offer the opportunity for clergy to mix and learn with those preparing for teaching and the caring professions, and to prepare to be effective in schools. At the same time, the ordinands would add significantly to the worship and Christian life of the colleges.

# Annex: the distinctiveness of Church colleges: a suggested framework

1. A Church of England college of higher education might be expected to offer:

    - courses in teacher education including specialist religious education;
    - courses relating to the needs of other caring professions;
    - courses in Christian theology and Church education;
    - courses leading to the Church Colleges' Certificates.

    In its initial teacher education courses, the college should:

    - meet at the highest possible quality the requirements relating to religious education, spiritual and moral development, and collective worship;
    - inform students about Church schools and give students the opportunity to undertake teaching practice and to prepare for careers in Church schools;
    - encourage all students to see teaching as a vocation.

    In its continuing professional development courses, the college might be expected to:

    - provide for the needs of headteachers, teachers and governors of Church schools;
    - provide for the needs of Christian teachers in all schools.

    In all its courses, the college might be expected to offer opportunities for students:

    - to develop the ability and commitment to contribute to the improvement of the human condition;
    - to consider matters relating to values and insights from Christian scholarship relevant to their subject area.

2. With regard to the educational context which it offers, the Church college should be a community:

    - which is welcoming, caring and supportive;
    - which displays values of honesty, openness, friendliness, trust and respect;
    - in which all students and staff are valued as individuals and helped to reach their full potential;
    - which recognizes and tries to meet responsibilities to serve those in need in the wider community and to act as stewards of creation;
    - which is committed to strive for excellence in all that it does.

    The community should:

    - be based on Christian principles;
    - provide opportunities for Christian worship;
    - offer a Christian influence to all its members.

**3.** The purposes of the Church colleges should reflect their Christian foundation and their response to the great commandments to love God and to love one's neighbour as oneself. Among other things the colleges should seek to:

- help all students to reach their full potential as complete and individual human beings;

- provide an education which stretches the mind, strengthens the body, enriches the imagination, nourishes the spirit, encourages the will to do good and opens the heart to others;

- develop in all students a sense of vocation.

**4.** As Christian institutions, the colleges might also be expected to respond in particular ways to the needs of groups of stakeholders, including students, the Church and society. For example, with respect to students, the Church college should make special provision for:

- Christian students;

- students from developing countries and from sections of society which have been traditionally underrepresented in higher education, including those with disabilities and those from minority ethnic groups.

The Church college might also be expected to help to meet the needs of the Church and especially the Anglican Church by:

- making available human and material resources;

- educating and training teachers for Church schools;

- supporting governors and clergy and members of faith communities at national, diocesan and parish level in meeting their responsibilities for Church schools;

- contributing to theological training for lay people, readers and the ordained ministry;

- playing a role in evangelism and in ecumenism.

In addition the Church college might be expected to respond to the needs of society by:

- preparing students to serve in the teaching and the caring professions;

- providing opportunities for continuing professional development in those areas;

- making available its resources to the community.

chapter 10
# Summary of recommendations

Strategic recommendations are shown in **bold**. Recommendations concerning good practice are shown in *italics*.

## Recommendations to the Archbishops' Council

- The Council should lead the Church in considering afresh how all elements in the Church – parishes, schools, dioceses, Church colleges and theological colleges, courses and schemes – can work more closely together in true partnership so that each can contribute more fully to the well-being of the others and realize the opportunities before us (1.6–1.9).

- The Council should review annually progress in implementing our recommendations for increasing the number of secondary places by the equivalent of 100 schools over the next seven to eight years (5.21).

- The Council should be instrumental in launching a national appeal to raise £25 million over a period of seven years to support dioceses in the proposed expansion of Church secondary provision (5.27–5.31).

- The Council should encourage and facilitate a structured approach in the dioceses to post-ordination training of clergy, which involves the Church colleges of higher education, and which equips clergy to be an effective and welcome presence in Church schools and more widely in Community schools (7.21–7.23).

## Recommendations to dioceses
### (a) Relationships

- All parishes with a Church school should review the relationship between the incumbent, the worshipping community and the Church school so that the school is in fact at the centre of the Church's mission (1.8 and 7.8).

- *The clergy appointments procedure should ensure that, where there is a Church school in the parish, prospective clergy are given a job description that makes explicit their responsibilities towards that school (7.8).*

- *The headteacher of the Church school should be involved in the welcome and induction of a new cleric (7.8).*

- *The parish church should welcome and celebrate the arrival of a new headteacher to its school (7.8).*

- *Whether or not the Chair of the governors of the Church school, the incumbent should always be involved in the selection of a new head and new teaching staff (7.8).*

- *Where it is the practice for the parish to be involved in the appointment of a new incumbent, the headteacher of the Church school in the parish should be involved (7.8).*

- *Dioceses should be ready to assist clergy and school heads if the relationship between school and parish is in disrepair (7.8).*

- *Dioceses should arrange for new headteachers to come together to review their experiences after three months, and if they wish it, an experienced head should be a guide, counsellor and friend in the first year.*

### (b) Religious education

- Dioceses should agree objectives with schools to raise standards of teaching, learning and achievement in religious education (4.12).

### (c) Partnership with Local Education Authorities

- Dioceses should continue to work in close partnership with LEAs, recognizing that this is fundamental to the well-being of Church schools.

- In advancing proposals for increased provision, dioceses should proceed in partnership as set out in Chapter 5.

### (d) Categories of Church school

- As now, Voluntary Aided and Voluntary Controlled and Foundation schools should rank equally in the care of the Church (4.18).

- When new Church schools are under consideration, the normal preference should be for a Voluntary Aided school, if financial circumstances allow and there is local agreement (4.21).

- *Voluntary Controlled schools should, from time to time, review their distinctiveness as Christian institutions and consider whether their local circumstances allow a legitimate case to be made to the LEA for the inclusion of Christian background within the admissions criteria, providing this does not compromise their tradition and responsibility as a neighbourhood school (4.40).*

### (e) Increased provision

- The Church should aim to increase Church secondary school places, whether by the expansion of existing schools or through additional Church schools (including transfers from the Community sector), by the equivalent of 100 schools over the next seven to eight years (5.21).

- In relation to this national objective, each diocese should consider what can be achieved over the next five years, and roll forward its thinking annually by a further year (5.21).

- In increasing provision the Church should see it as part of its special mission to serve the most disadvantaged in society and children with special educational needs (5.21).

- The Church should foster an ecumenical approach where this is appropriate (5.21)

- At the primary level, dioceses should aim to increase provision where it is most evidently lacking (5.21).

### (f) Caring for teachers and developing potential headteachers

- The Church should see it as a direct responsibility to raise the respect for, and the morale of, teachers. Church schools should stand out as places where teachers and other staff are valued and respected. The headteacher should be able to look to the parish church as a source of unfailing support and encouragement. Governors, particularly the Chair, as well as the parish and the diocese all have a part to play. It is their business to know the headteacher, to help, to sustain and to encourage (6.5).

- *Being a school governor should be recognized as one of the most important roles a Church member can take (6.6).*

- It must be seen as a major concern of the Church at national and diocesan level to identify, develop and recruit committed leaders from Christian teachers in all schools (6.16).

- Action must be taken now to identify on a national basis, diocese by diocese, Christian teachers of all ages, young and old, who have the potential to provide the necessary leadership. The dioceses must see that these teachers have the in-service development needed to move on to senior positions (6.18).

- Through the dioceses, all parishes should be urged, not just once but repeatedly, to put before people what it means to be a Christian teacher and, in appropriate cases, encourage a vocation to teach (6.26).

- *The Church should affirm Christian teachers through pastoral visits to schools by the archbishops and bishops and through inviting Christian teachers in Church and Community schools, including Special schools, to appropriate events organized with the bishop. Dioceses should work towards greater involvement in supporting associations of Christian teachers (6.34).*

- *Dioceses should show the importance the Church attributes to the appointment of headteachers by a Service of Commissioning of the kind that has been agreed in some dioceses (6.34).*

- *Diocesan vocations advisers should encourage a vocation to teach as well as to the ordained ministry (6.34).*

### (g) Admissions Policies

- *Voluntary Aided schools must comply with the Code of Practice on School Admissions, ensuring that admission criteria are clear, objective and fair (4.47).*

- *All dioceses should adopt the policy already employed by many dioceses of offering guidance to schools on their Admissions Policy (4.47).*

- *Voluntary Aided schools should aim to offer some places as a high priority to children with special educational or medical needs, as representing the Church's commitment to those most in need (4.47).*

- *All Church schools should consider how they are responding to the changing needs of the local community (4.47).*

- In any new primary and secondary schools it should be the policy to establish within measurable time – if it is not possible from the outset – at least a substantial minority of pupils with a Christian background (4.47).

- In particular, the aim over time in new Voluntary Aided schools should be to achieve an appropriate balance of 'open' and 'foundation' places, sufficient to ensure that the school is a distinctively Christian institution whilst remaining grounded in the local community in all its diversity (4.47).

### (h) Anglican independent schools

- Anglican independent schools should always be considered as part of the family of Church schools, and opportunities should be taken to foster the relations between maintained and independent schools (4.57).

- The Church should always be mindful of the independent Anglican schools in its stewardship at national and diocesan level, and should consciously pursue a policy of inclusiveness through the development of bi-lateral relationships between independent and maintained schools (4.57).

- The independent schools in a diocese should be invited to propose a member for the Diocesan Board of Education, and reciprocally bishops should canvass the possibility of a DBE representative or other nominee of the bishop becoming a member of the governing body of independent schools (4.57).

### (i) Diocesan structures

- *Dioceses should reflect on the benefit to be gained from a single structure for education and training (8.12– 8.13).*

- *Diocesan boards of education should consider the adoption of a national model for their accountability, put into practice in consultation with National Society/Church of England Board of Education officers (8.16).*

- Dioceses should consider some increased resources for diocesan boards of education in giving effect to the recommendations in this report, notably through arrangements organized on a regional basis through the dioceses themselves, and with the help of funding obtained through the national fundraising proposal in this report (5.27).

## Recommendations to parishes and deaneries

- *Headteachers, or other suitable teachers, should have the opportunity to talk regularly to PCCs. Indeed, where possible, the headteacher should be a valued member of the PCC (6.10).*

- The Church should find new ways of encouraging the recruitment of teachers from minority ethnic groups, and encourage more men to offer themselves for teaching in primary schools (6.20).

- *Education Sunday should be celebrated in all parishes and the service should actively involve Christian teachers (6.34).*

- *Parishes and schools should pray regularly for each other (1.8 and 7.8).*

- All parishes, and all Church schools, should reflect on the implications of the General Synod Resolution that Church schools are at the centre of the Church's mission in terms of their own parish and their own school (7.8).

- Deaneries should be active in fostering the kind of relationships between parishes and Church schools implicit in the General Synod's Resolution identifying Church schools at the centre of the Church's mission to the nation (1.6 – 1.8 and 7.4 – 7.8).

- *Deaneries and parishes should ensure that the Local Education Authority's child protection policy is in place and that appropriate training has been provided for the clergy and lay people involved in school ministry (7.8).*

## Recommendations to schools and school governors
### (a) The character of Church schools

- Where they have not already done so, governing bodies in all Church schools should consider adopting the ethos statement as set out in paragraph 3.24 of the report and as a minimum adopt the practices relating to Christian distinctiveness detailed in paragraph 4.6 of the report, to which we refer you.

### (b) Religious education

- *All Church secondary schools should expect that pupils should take at least the short course GCSE and preferably the full GCSE in religious studies (4.13).*

- *Church secondary schools with sixth forms should offer A and AS Level courses in RE, and encourage students to take these courses (4.13).*

### (c) Helping the Church in its task to raise the respect for, and morale of teachers

- *Governors should see it as a core part of their role to relate personally to all members of staff individually (6.7).*

- *Governors should encourage parents to show their appreciation of the work of teachers by expressing thanks and showing that they value the care which teachers are taking to benefit the children (6.8).*

- *Governing bodies should be vigilant to see that the headteachers in small schools do not exhaust themselves by taking a greater teaching load than they should, and also to see that they take proper opportunities for professional development (6.23).*

- *School governors and headteachers should keep in touch with teachers from the school who have left the profession before retirement so that they may feel encouraged to return (6.11).*

### (d) The vocation to teach

- Christian teachers should encourage suitable pupils to think of teaching as a vocation and, if it seems right for the pupils, encourage them to think of going to a Church college for their higher education and their teaching qualification (6.34).

### (e) Admissions Policies

- *Voluntary Controlled primary schools serving a village community should remain as primarily to serve those communities, but in so doing they should always be and be seen to be distinctively Christian institutions (4.5).*

- *In framing their Admissions Policies, Voluntary Aided primary schools that historically have served the local community should have clear admissions criteria which give an order of priority and take into account the school's purposes as set out in the original trust deed. Where there is long-term oversubscription, governors should consider whether an enlargement of the school is possible (4.41).*

- *Governing bodies of Voluntary Aided secondary schools in areas where there are several secondary schools may justifiably conclude that the task of the school is to nurture Anglican or other Christian children in their faith and allocate places accordingly. They should, however, reserve places for children of other faiths and of no faith (4.44).*

### (f) Parents and Church schools

- *It should be a special objective of every Church school to engage the parents in the education and the broader school life of the child (3.10).*

## Recommendations to Church colleges

- *We invite the Anglican Church colleges to continue working together to develop the Church Colleges' Certificates in Church School Studies or Religious Studies and the award of credits towards professional qualifications (6.31).*

- *The Church Colleges' Certificates in Church School Studies and in Religious Studies should be made available by the colleges on a national basis, both through college courses and distance learning, and dioceses should actively encourage the take up of these qualifications by practising teachers as well as by entrants to the profession (6.34).*

- We recommend that the Church colleges and dioceses should establish a small working group to recommend action now to identify best practice for developing relationships between the colleges and all dioceses, whether they have a Church college or not (9.15).

- We recommend that the eight colleges that do not have degree awarding powers should seek them and support one another in the relevant applications (9.20).

- Where the viability of a Church college becomes in doubt, we urge that the college gives early and serious consideration to a merger or other form of partnership with another Church college. We further recommend that in view of the distinctive contribution of the Church colleges to the provision of education in schools that the Teacher Training Agency and the Higher Education Funding Council provide appropriate transitional support to facilitate such a merger. We invite the Church at national level to pursue this matter with Government (9.34).

- We recommend that the Church should develop a strategic view of its relationships with the colleges and that the Church should affirm the essential role of the colleges through using the colleges as the first source of relevant advice on relevant matters. We also invite the Church to consider what long-term role the Church colleges might have in the pre- and post-ordination training of the clergy (9.40).

- Finally, we attach much importance to the distinctiveness of the Church colleges and offer as an annex to chapter 9 a suggested framework.

## Recommendations to theological colleges, courses and schemes

- Recognizing the pressures on the curricula of the theological colleges, courses and schemes, most of the training of clergy for work in Church schools will need to be post-ordination, but we offer consideration that initial ministerial education should offer ordinands:

    a basic understanding of the ecclesiology and missiology of Church schools and their legal basis;

    wherever possible brief placements – arranged during the school term – during pre-ordination training in a parish with a Church school or failing that in a parish with a Community school where the incumbent is active;

    where the pre-ordination programme covers two or more academic years a module on Church schools, where this can reasonably be offered as an option to supplement the basic curriculum (7.20).

- The focus of post-ordination training in relation to schools must be strongly developed. It needs to be structured by the dioceses and should sensibly involve the Church colleges of higher education (7.21).

## Recommendations to the Church of England Board of Education and National Society

- The Church at national level should see it as one of its prime responsibilities to work with the Government to achieve a reduction in the personal administrative load on the heads of small primary schools to a realistic level (6.24).

- Materials should be prepared to help all those who have the opportunity to encourage people to consider teaching as a professional vocation (6.34).

- The Church should work for the greater recognition and status of RE teachers in all schools by the provision of an appropriate career structure and corresponding salary scales and resources (6.32).

## Proposals to Government and Government Agencies

- There should be continued action to reduce the flow of paper and reduce the administrative load on the heads of small primary schools (6.21– 6.24 and 8.6).

- The setting up of a 'small schools unit' with involvement by LEAs and the voluntary sector should be considered with a view to identifying and fostering arrangements for reducing the administrative load on small schools (6.24).

- In teacher training, in a revision of DfEE Circular 4/98, appropriate coverage should be given to values, virtues and purposes (9.23).

- The National College for School Leadership should include provision for the particular dimension of leadership in faith-based schools within the framework of the National Professional Qualification for Headship (6.18).

- The Teacher Training Agency and the Higher Education Funding Council should provide appropriate transitional support to facilitate merger of Church colleges when their viability comes into doubt (9.34).

*appendix 1*
# Differences between categories of Church schools

|  | Voluntary Aided schools | Voluntary Controlled schools | Foundation schools |
|---|---|---|---|
| **Buildings** | Owned by trustees: The trust deed determines the basis on which the school is run. New building and external repairs are the responsibility of the governors (supported by grant from the DfEE up to 85% of approval expenditure). [90% grant now proposed.] Playing fields are provided by the LEA. | Owned by trustees. The trust deed determines how the school shall be run where the law does not make this clear. All replacement, repairs and other building costs fall on the LEA. | Owned by trustees. The trust deed determines the basis on which the school shall be run where the law is silent. Playing fields owned by governors. All building works funded from LEA. |
| **Staff (a) Teaching** | Employed by the governors, paid by the LEA. Governors may seek evidence of Christian commitment from applications for teaching posts. | Appointed by the governors, employed and paid by the LEA. Governors are bound by LEA appointing policies. Governors will be able to satisfy themselves that a candidate for the post of headteacher is suitable to support and develop the ethos of a Voluntary Controlled school. | Employed by the governors, paid by the LEA. Governors will be able to select teachers within the LEA policy. Governors are bound by LEA appointing policies. Governors will be able to satisfy themselves that a candidate for the post of headteacher is suitable to support and develop the ethos of a Foundation school. |
| **Staff (b) support** | Employed either by governors or contractors. If employed by governors they are paid by LEA. | Employed either by LEA or contractors. LEA employees usually appointed by governors. | Employed either by governors or contractors. If employed by governors they are paid by LEA. |
| **Worship** | Reflects the Anglican tradition and can include worship in the parish church. | Reflects the Anglican tradition and can include worship in the parish church. | Reflects Anglican tradition and can include worship in the parish church. |

Appendix 1

| | | | |
|---|---|---|---|
| RE | Governors determine a syllabus that reflects the Anglican traditions. They may make use of the diocesan syllabus where this exists. | The school must follow the LEA syllabus unless the parents request a denominational one. The foundation governors have rights in the appointment of staff (called reserved teachers) to teach denominational RE. | The school must follow the LEA syllabus unless the parents request a denominational one. The foundation governors have rights in the appointment of staff (called reserved teachers) to teach denominational RE. |
| Membership of the Governing body | Church (foundation) governors have an absolute majority over all other governors. Parish priest is usually *ex officio* a member of the governing body. All governors combine to elect the Chair. A proportion of foundation governors must also be parents. | Church (foundation) governors are in a minority. The parish priest is usually *ex officio* a member of the governing body. All governors combine to elect the Chair. | Church (foundation) governors are in a minority. The parish priest is usually *ex officio* a member of the governing body. All governors combine to elect the Chair. |
| Funding | LEA LMS formula. Governors' costs for building work from locally raised funds, PCCs, local trusts and, usually, trusts administered by the dioceses. | LEA LMS formula. | LEA LMS formula. |
| Admissions | Governors determine the policy and make the decisions. They must consult the LEA and all other admission authorities in the area each year. | The LEA is responsible for admissions, but must consult the governing body each year. | Governors determine the policy and make the decisions. They must consult the LEA and all other admission authorities in the area each year. |
| Advice | LEA Chief Education Officer has certain rights to attend governor meetings to give advice. Diocesan directors of education have parallel rights. | LEA Chief Education Officer has certain rights to attend governor meetings to give advice. Governors may give similar rights to the diocesan director of education. | LEA Chief Education Officer has certain rights to attend governor meetings to give advice. Governors may give similar rights to the diocesan director of education. |
| Inspection | OFSTED/ESTYN inspectors look at most issues. Section 23 inspectors inspect RE, worship and school ethos. | OFSTED/ESTYN inspectors look at general issues and RE. Section 23 inspectors inspect worship and may report on ethos. | OFSTED/ESTYN inspectors look at general issues and RE. Section 23 inspectors inspect worship and may report on ethos. |

*appendix 2*
# Church Schools by diocese

## CHURCH OF ENGLAND SECONDARY SCHOOLS BY DIOCESE

| DIOCESE | Primary | | | | Middle Deemed Primary | | | | TOTAL PRIMARY |
|---|---|---|---|---|---|---|---|---|---|
| | VA | VC | F | Total | VA | VC | F | Total | |
| BATH AND WELLS | 43 | 129 | 1 | 173 | | | | | 173 |
| BIRMINGHAM | 25 | 25 | | 50 | | | | | 50 |
| BLACKBURN | 152 | 27 | | 179 | | | | | 179 |
| BRADFORD | 26 | 31 | 3 | 60 | | | | | 60 |
| BRISTOL | 9 | 56 | 1 | 66 | | | | | 66 |
| CANTERBURY | 27 | 73 | | 100 | | | | | 100 |
| CARLISLE | 52 | 52 | 6 | 110 | | | | | 110 |
| CHELMSFORD | 60 | 67 | 6 | 133 | | | | | 133 |
| CHESTER | 53 | 61 | | 114 | | | | | 114 |
| CHICHESTER | 51 | 94 | | 145 | 4 | 1 | | 5 | 150 |
| COVENTRY | 23 | 49 | 1 | 73 | | | | | 73 |
| DERBY | 32 | 77 | | 109 | | | | | 109 |
| DURHAM | 18 | 35 | | 53 | | | | | 53 |
| ELY | 29 | 52 | | 81 | | | | | 81 |
| EXETER | 54 | 72 | | 126 | 3 | 1 | | 4 | 130 |
| GLOUCESTER | 43 | 72 | 2 | 117 | | | | | 117 |
| GUILDFORD | 48 | 33 | 1 | 82 | | | | | 82 |
| HEREFORD | 37 | 48 | | 85 | | | | | 85 |
| LEICESTER | 21 | 73 | | 94 | | | | | 94 |
| LICHFIELD | 45 | 160 | 2 | 207 | | | | | 207 |
| LINCOLN | 31 | 103 | 6 | 140 | | | | | 140 |
| LIVERPOOL | 78 | 36 | | 114 | | | | | 114 |
| LONDON | 130 | 1 | | 131 | 1 | | | 1 | 132 |
| MANCHESTER | 102 | 86 | 1 | 189 | | | | | 189 |
| NEWCASTLE | 31 | 9 | | 40 | | | | | 40 |
| NORWICH | 36 | 63 | 1 | 100 | 1 | 10 | 1 | 12 | 112 |
| OXFORD | 80 | 182 | | 262 | 1 | | | 1 | 263 |
| PETERBOROUGH | 28 | 70 | 1 | 99 | | | | | 99 |
| PORTSMOUTH | 10 | 35 | | 45 | | | | | 45 |
| RIPON AND LEEDS | 28 | 66 | | 94 | | | | | 94 |
| ROCHESTER | 28 | 53 | 1 | 82 | | | | | 82 |
| SALISBURY | 85 | 102 | 1 | 188 | 1 | 2 | | 3 | 191 |
| SHEFFIELD | 34 | 8 | | 42 | | | | | 42 |
| SODOR AND MAN | | 1 | | 1 | | | | | 1 |
| SOUTHWARK | 86 | 5 | 1 | 92 | 1 | | | 1 | 93 |
| SOUTHWELL | 31 | 34 | | 65 | | | | | 65 |
| ST ALBANS | 71 | 53 | | 124 | | | | | 124 |
| ST E AND I | 17 | 68 | | 85 | 2 | 2 | | 4 | 89 |
| TRURO | 36 | 12 | | 48 | | | | | 48 |
| WAKEFIELD | 44 | 55 | | 99 | | 1 | | 1 | 100 |
| WINCHESTER | 38 | 56 | | 94 | | | | | 94 |
| WORCESTER | 26 | 67 | | 93 | | | | | 93 |
| YORK | 18 | 103 | 3 | 124 | | | | | 124 |
| TOTAL | 1916 | 2554 | 38 | 4508 | 14 | 17 | 1 | 32 | 4540 |

## CHURCH IN WALES SCHOOLS BY DIOCESE

| DIOCESE | Primary | | | |
|---|---|---|---|---|
| | VA | VC | F | Total |
| BANGOR | 1 | 18 | | 19 |
| LLANDAFF | 19 | 5 | | 24 |
| MONMOUTH | 7 | 12 | | 19 |
| ST ASAPH | 20 | 34 | | 54 |
| ST DAVIDS | 8 | 32 | | 40 |
| SWANSEA AND BRECON | 6 | 13 | | 19 |
| TOTAL | 61 | 114 | | 175 |

### KEY

| | |
|---|---|
| VA | Voluntary Aided |
| VC | Voluntary Controlled |
| F | Foundation |

*This list has been compiled by the National Society in consultation with dioceses.*

Appendix 2

## CHURCH OF ENGLAND SECONDARY SCHOOLS BY DIOCESE

| DIOCESE | Secondary | | | | | Middle Deemed Secondary | | | | TOTAL SECONDARY | Independent Schools |
|---|---|---|---|---|---|---|---|---|---|---|---|
| | VA | VC | F | CTC | Total | VA | VC | F | Total | | |
| BATH AND WELLS | 3 | 3 | | | 6 | | 3 | | 3 | 9 | 7 |
| BIRMINGHAM | 1 | 1 | | | 2 | | | | | 2 | 2 |
| BLACKBURN | 8 | 1 | | | 9 | | | | | 9 | 4 |
| BRADFORD | 2 | | | | 2 | | 1 | | 1 | 3 | 2 |
| BRISTOL | 1 | | | | 1 | | | | | 1 | 2 |
| CANTERBURY | 1 | | 2 | | 3 | 1 | | | 1 | 4 | 9 |
| CARLISLE | 2 | | | | 2 | | | | | 2 | 4 |
| CHELMSFORD | 1 | 1 | | | 2 | | | | | 2 | 6 |
| CHESTER | 1 | | | | 1 | | | | | 1 | 6 |
| CHICHESTER | 4 | 3 | | | 7 | | | | | 7 | 12 |
| COVENTRY | 2 | | | | 2 | | | | | 2 | 3 |
| DERBY | | | | | | | | | | | 5 |
| DURHAM | 1 | | | | 1 | | | | | 1 | 3 |
| ELY | 1 | | | | 1 | | | | | 1 | 2 |
| EXETER | 1 | 1 | | | 2 | | | | | 2 | 9 |
| GLOUCESTER | | | | | | | | | | | 5 |
| GUILDFORD | 2 | 1 | | | 3 | | | | | 3 | 16 |
| HEREFORD | 1 | 1 | | | 2 | | | | | 2 | 3 |
| LEICESTER | | 3 | | | 3 | | | | | 3 | 2 |
| LICHFIELD | 4 | | | | 4 | 2 | 4 | | 6 | 10 | 8 |
| LINCOLN | | 2 | 3 | | 5 | | | | | 5 | 2 |
| LIVERPOOL | 4 | | | | 4 | | | | | 4 | 1 |
| LONDON | 16 | | | | 16 | | | | | 16 | 14 |
| MANCHESTER | 7 | 2 | | | 9 | | | | | 9 | 1 |
| NEWCASTLE | | | | | | 2 | | | 2 | 2 | 4 |
| NORWICH | 1 | | | | 1 | | | | | 1 | 4 |
| OXFORD | 2 | 4 | | | 6 | 3 | 2 | | 5 | 11 | 30 |
| PETERBOROUGH | 2 | | 1 | | 3 | 2 | | | 2 | 5 | 7 |
| PORTSMOUTH | 1 | | | | 1 | 1 | 2 | | 3 | 4 | |
| RIPON AND LEEDS | 4 | | | | 4 | | | | | 4 | 5 |
| ROCHESTER | 4 | | | | 4 | | | | | 4 | 3 |
| SALISBURY | 3 | 6 | 1 | | 10 | 4 | 5 | | 9 | 19 | 11 |
| SHEFFIELD | | | | | | | | | | | |
| SODOR AND MAN | | | | | | | | | | | 1 |
| SOUTHWARK | 11 | 1 | | 1 | 13 | | | | | 13 | 15 |
| SOUTHWELL | 3 | 1 | | | 4 | 1 | | | 1 | 5 | 2 |
| ST ALBANS | 3 | 1 | | | 4 | 4 | 3 | | 7 | 11 | 12 |
| ST E AND I | | 2 | | | 2 | 6 | 1 | | 7 | 9 | 4 |
| TRURO | | | | | | | | | | | 2 |
| WAKEFIELD | 1 | 1 | | | 2 | | | | | 2 | 2 |
| WINCHESTER | | | | | | | | | | | 11 |
| WORCESTER | 2 | | | | 2 | 1 | 9 | 1 | 11 | 13 | 9 |
| YORK | 1 | 2 | | | 3 | | | | | 3 | 5 |
| TOTAL | 101 | 37 | 7 | 1 | 146 | 27 | 30 | 1 | 58 | 204 | 255 |

## CHURCH IN WALES SCHOOLS BY DIOCESE

| DIOCESE | Secondary | | | | | Indep. |
|---|---|---|---|---|---|---|
| | VA | VC | F | CTC | Total | |
| BANGOR | | | | | | |
| LLANDAFF | 3 | | | | 3 | |
| MONMOUTH | | | | | | |
| ST ASAPH | | | | | | 2 |
| ST DAVIDS | | | | | | |
| SWANSEA AND BRECON | | | | | | 4 |
| TOTAL | 3 | | | | 3 | 6 |

### KEY

| | |
|---|---|
| VA | Voluntary Aided |
| VC | Voluntary Controlled |
| F | Foundation |
| CTC | City Technology College |

*This list has been compiled by the National Society in consultation with dioceses.*

*appendix 3*
# Church of England secondary school GCSE results and other statistics

Research undertaken for the Review Group showed that looking at average GCSE point scores at the aggregate level of LEAs, Church of England secondary school GCSE results were about 12 per cent higher than the results for all maintained schools in LEA areas:

### LEA average GCSE point scores in 1999 and 2000

|  | 1999 | 2000 |
|---|---|---|
| Church of England schools | 41.1 | 42 |
| All LEA schools * | 36.8 | 37.6 |

(* includes **all** maintained schools in each local education authority area including special schools and city technology colleges)

Source of data: DfEE website

An analysis of standards in Church schools provided by Dr John Marks for the research institute Civitas, who submitted evidence to the Review Group, showed that the percentage of pupils achieving five or more A*–C GCSE passes in Church of England and Community schools is as follows:

### Percentage of pupils in Church of England and Community secondary schools achieving five or more A*–C passes at GCSE

|  | Percentage achieving 5+ A*–C Passes | Number of Schools |
|---|---|---|
| **Comprehensive schools** |  |  |
| Church of England schools | 50.8% | 128 |
| Community schools | 41.8% | 2204 |
| **Secondary modern schools** |  |  |
| Church of England schools | 36.3% | 7 |
| Community schools | 30.9% | 139 |
| **Grammar schools** |  |  |
| Church of England schools | 99.0% | 4 |
| Community schools | 95.0% | 91 |

At A Level, the analysis by Dr Marks showed very little difference in results between Church of England and Community schools.

Appendix 3

The following tables illustrate our own analysis, based on OFSTED data for individual Church schools, of the performance of Church of England secondary schools, together with some other useful statistics.

### Church of England secondary school statistics
### Average GCSE point scores

|         | 1998 | 1999 | 2000 |
|---------|------|------|------|
| Mean    | 39.2 | 40.5 | 41.1 |
| Median  | 39.0 | 40.8 | 42.1 |
| Highest | 63.5 | 64.5 | 65.1 |
| Lowest  | 15.6 | 14.7 | 15.5 |

### Percentage of pupils with English as an additional language (#)

|        | 1998 | 1999 | 2000  |
|--------|------|------|-------|
| Mean   | 8.3% | 8.6% | 10.0% |
| Median | 1.2% | 1.2% | 1.5%  |

### Percentage of pupils with special needs

|        | 1998  | 1999  | 2000  |
|--------|-------|-------|-------|
| Mean   | 18.1% | 18.9% | 19.9% |
| Median | 16.3% | 16.4% | 16.5% |

### Percentage of pupils with statements of special needs

|        | 1998 | 1999 | 2000 |
|--------|------|------|------|
| Mean   | 2.3% | 2.3% | 2.5% |
| Median | 2.0% | 2.0% | 1.9% |

(#) N.B. The large difference between the mean and the median (percentage of pupils with English as an additional language) is because a small number of schools have a very high proportion of pupils in this category.

The proportion of free school meals is often taken as an indicator of the social background of parents (although some have questioned this measure). An analysis by the Review Group, based on OFSTED data, has shown that an average of 14.9 per cent of children in Church of England secondary schools were eligible for free school meals over the three years 1998–2000 compared with an overall England average of 17 per cent over the same period.

## OFSTED inspection data

OFSTED provided the Review Group with inspection data for 133 Church of England secondary schools. Of these, 34 were given a 'Very Good' rating, 62 were given a 'Good' rating, 29 were given a 'Satisfactory' rating and 8 were given an 'Unsatisfactory' rating.

We are most grateful to OFSTED for supplying the base statistics for us to analyse.

*appendix 4*
# Anglican colleges in England and Wales

| College | Location | Foundation and date | Validating body |
|---|---|---|---|
| Bishop Grosseteste College | Lincoln | Bishop Grosseteste, 1862 | University of Hull |
| Canterbury Christ Church University College | Canterbury Tonbridge | Canterbury Christ Church, 1962 | Degree awarding |
| Cheltenham and Gloucester College of Higher Education | Cheltenham | St Paul's, 1847 St Mary's, 1850 | Degree awarding |
| Chester College of Higher Education | Chester | Chester College, 1839 | University of Liverpool |
| University College Chichester | Chichester | Bishop Otter College, 1840 | Degree awarding |
| King Alfred's College, Winchester | Winchester | King Alfred's College, 1840 | University of Southampton |
| Liverpool Hope College | Liverpool | St Katherine's 1844 | University of Liverpool |
| College of Ripon and York St John | York Ripon | St. John's, York, 1841 Ripon, 1861 | University of Leeds |
| University of Surrey Roehampton | Wandsworth, SW London | Whitelands College, 1842 | Degree awarding |
| College of St. Mark and St John | Plymouth | St John's, 1840 St Mark's, 1841 | University of Exeter |
| St Martin's College | Lancaster Ambleside Carlisle | St Martin's College, 1963 | University of Lancaster |
| Trinity College, Carmarthen | Carmarthen | Trinity College, 1848 | University of Wales |

## NUMBERS OF STUDENTS IN THE ANGLICAN COLLEGES OF HIGHER EDUCATION 1999-2000

| | Total HE Students 1999-2000 | Total HE Students in Education | Percent in Education | Full-Time UG Total | Full-Time UG Education | Percent in Education | Full-Time PGT | Full-Time PGT Education | Percent in Education |
|---|---|---|---|---|---|---|---|---|---|
| Bishop Grosseteste | 1,000 | 850 | 85% | 770 | 630 | 82% | 20 | 20 | 100% |
| Canterbury Christ Church University College | 10,520 | 3,410 | 32% | 4,400 | 650 | 15% | 630 | 460 | 73% |
| Cheltenham and Gloucester | 8,040 | 760 | 9% | 5,570 | 410 | 7% | 320 | 210 | 66% |
| Chester College | 6,420 | 800 | 12% | 3,430 | 420 | 12% | 170 | 80 | 47% |
| University College Chichester | 3,490 | 1,030 | 30% | 2,600 | 790 | 30% | 150 | 130 | 87% |
| King Alfred's College | 4,870 | 1,410 | 29% | 3,020 | 960 | 32% | 90 | 50 | 56% |
| Liverpool Hope | 5,530 | 1,180 | 21% | 3,550 | 750 | 21% | 340 | 240 | 71% |
| College of Ripon and York St John | 4,120 | 1,230 | 30% | 2,970 | 900 | 30% | 170 | 150 | 88% |
| University of Surrey Roehampton | 7,240 | 1,970 | 27% | 5,260 | 1,000 | 19% | 550 | 420 | 76% |
| College of St Mark and St John | 3,180 | 1,990 | 63% | 2,260 | 1,180 | 52% | 270 | 240 | 89% |
| St Martin's College | 7,600 | 2,780 | 37% | 3,670 | 1,430 | 39% | 530 | 510 | 96% |
| Trinity College Carmarthen | 1,660 | 590 | 36% | 1,100 | 460 | 42% | 150 | 110 | 73% |
| Total | 63,670 | 18,000 | 28% | 38,600 | 9,580 | 25% | 3,390 | 2,620 | 77% |

Total HE Students includes part-time students.

Source: HESA: Students in Higher Education Institutions 1999/2000, tables 8a, 8c and 8g

**Key**
HE : Higher Education
UG : Undergraduates
PGT : Postgraduate Taught Courses

*appendix 5*
# Vocation
## by the Archbishop of Wales

In the most general sense, vocation is God's summons into existence itself. God calls creation into being; every thing that is made is called and named; its identity lies in the purposive call of God. But for the Christian, this is more specific again: human beings are called to grow in community into the likeness of Jesus Christ. Their vocation is not just to exist, but to come into a life that shares in Christ's life. The Church's very name (*ekklesia*) means 'a community that is called together'; but the Church is not only a called community, it is a community that represents God's call and invitation to all humanity.

So specific 'vocations' within the Church need to be seen as ways of representing and reinforcing this basic invitation from God; vocation in the Church reminds the world that it is called into being and invited into new being. Particular styles of life and ministry in the Church are different ways of echoing God's call.

In this light, we need to be careful about separating person from function. Only when I am conscious of being called by God to be myself in Christ can I find what specific work he asks of me in passing on that discovery and that hope to others. If we bear the call of God to others, that will itself be a way of becoming more profoundly who we are and who we are meant to be.

It is possible to see the whole of the educational process as a story of vocation, to the extent that it is about *inviting* people to become what they can be. Christian education will be particularly attentive to this, always asking what it is that this or that person can show us of God's love and Christ's renewing power.

So, as with vocation in general, the process of education needs people who have some sense of being called and 'invited' themselves. It has long been recognized that the best teachers tend to be those who don't separate person and function, who find that encouraging others to respond to their fullest potential is what makes them themselves. This is an aspect of teaching very much obscured by all the trends in our society to regard teaching as simple communication of skills or information (not to mention the idea of replacing teachers by computers for certain purposes). Any Christian educational process ought to be fully conscious of this dimension, however, and should give priority in its vision to a very clear acknowledgement of the teacher's work as the way a teacher responds to God's call to become herself or himself in helping others to become themselves.

There are obvious implications for *all* teacher training, but especially Christian training. One of the areas for Church colleges to take on board is this question of personal nurture and development in 'becoming oneself in

Christ'. Chaplaincy in such an institution is not just liturgical or even pastoral; it needs to have some aspects of real spiritual stretching about it, what in ordination training would be called 'formation'. Likewise, professional development for the Christian teacher is something that must involve attention to the teacher's calling as disciple, as someone called to call others and open doors for their spiritual growth.

This task is not just for other educational professionals. Pastors and local church communities need to be involved in supporting and stretching the calling of the teachers in their schools and in their congregations. Teachers working in non-Church schools are likely to need as much or even more in the way of nurture, to sustain their awareness of their work as a calling.

In a school community, much depends in all this upon the skills of a headteacher. In the Church school, it is absolutely essential that a head should understand this vocational dimension to the staff's work (even in the case of those staff who have little or no overt religious commitment, but are willing to work for the school's ethos). The head needs to see that these issues of 'formation' and support for a vision that does not separate function and person are addressed in professional development programmes and so on. And if s/he is to do this effectively, s/he will need resourcing in turn. Christian heads require professional training that will keep before them the job of undergirding the vocational side of all the work of a school – as well as, once again, serious and sympathetic help from local congregations, and understanding from Foundation governors who can be relied on to support the vision.

In brief, a head who is conscious of this vision, and above all a head in a Church school, will be someone who is capable of resisting some of the pressures towards functionalism, crudely measurable outcomes and the depersonalizing of the teaching relationship that are around in the educational establishment.

*appendix 6*
# Membership of subgroups

The Chairman and Secretary of the Review Group were *ex-officio* members of each subgroup.

\* Denotes a Member of the Review Group or an Assessor.

## 1. Distinctiveness and the nature of the Church school

Mrs Julie Wilks* (Chair)

The Revd Professor Jeff Astley
(Director of the North of England Institute for Christian Education)

The Revd Canon Professor Leslie Francis
(Director of the Welsh National Centre for Religious Education and Professor of Practical Theology, University of Wales, Bangor)

Mr David Lankshear
(Schools Officer, Church of England Board of Education and Deputy General Secretary, National Society)

Mrs Margaret Nicholson (Secretary)
(Diocesan Director of Education, Diocese of Newcastle)

The Revd Peter Shepherd
(Headmaster of Canon Slade School, Bolton)

Professor Arthur Pollard*

## 2. Strategic development

Mr Peter Crook* (Chair)

Mrs Irene Bishop
(Headmistress of St Saviour's and St Olave's CE High School, London SE1)

The Revd Canon John Hall
(General Secretary of the Church of England Board of Education and National Society)

The Revd Andrew Martlew
(Diocesan Director of Education, Diocese of York)

Professor Arthur Pollard*

Mrs Linda Robinson
(Formerly Headteacher of St Wilfrid's CE High School and Technology College, Blackburn)

Appendix 6

## 3. Church schools in a pluralist society

Lord Dearing CB* (Chair)

Mr Alan Brown
(Schools Officer (RE), Church of England Board of Education and Deputy General Secretary, National Society)

Dr Priscilla Chadwick
(Principal of Berkhamsted Collegiate School)

Ms Margaret Ingram
(Deputy Principal of Hills Road Sixth Form College, Cambridge)

Mrs Lesley Morrison
(Headteacher of St Martin-in-the-Fields High School for Girls, London SW2)

Mrs Wendy Parmley
(Headteacher of Archbishop Michael Ramsey Technology College, London SE5)

Ms Jill Pauling
(Headteacher of St Philip's CE VA Primary School, Cambridge)

## 4. The relationship of the Church school to the parish

The Revd Peter Hill* (Chair)

Mr Alan Brown
(Schools Officer (RE), Church of England Board of Education and Deputy Secretary, National Society)

Mrs Paulette Bissell
(RE Adviser, Lincoln DBE)

The Revd Richard Lindley
(Diocesan Director of Education, Diocese of Winchester)

The Revd Howard Worsley
(Lecturer in Practical Theology, St John's College, Nottingham)

## 5. The legislative framework

Lord Dearing* (Chair)

Mr Peter Beesley
(Messrs Lee, Bolton & Lee)

Ms Daphne Griffith
(Education Administration Officer, Church of England Board of Education)

Mr Sydney Fremantle CBE (Secretary)
(Retired Civil Servant)

Mr Nick Richens
(Messrs Lee, Bolton & Lee)

The Revd Canon Tony Williamson
(Formerly Diocesan Director of Education, Diocese of Oxford)

## 6. LEA partnership

Ms Christine Whatford* (Chair)

Ms Liz Dobie
(Kirklees Metropolitan Council)

Ms Daphne Griffith
(Education Administration Officer, Church of England Board of Education)

Mr Michael Nix
(East Sussex County Council)

Professor Arthur Pollard*

## 7. Leadership, management and governance

Mrs Linda Borthwick* (Chair)

Dr Ruth Eade
(Adviser to Schools and Governors, Salisbury DBE)

Mr David Lankshear
(Schools Officer, Church of England Board of Education and Deputy General Secretary, National Society)

Mrs Oona Stannard*

## 8. The Church colleges

Dr John Rea* (Chair)

Dr Arthur Naylor
(Principal of St Mary's College, Twickenham)

Mr Richard Osmond (Secretary)
(Formerly Secretary of the Post Office, Governor of King Alfred's College, Winchester)

Mr Philip Robinson
(Director of University College, Chichester)

*appendix 7*
# Glossary of abbreviations and other terms

| | |
|---|---|
| CCC | Council of Church Colleges |
| CCRS | Catholic Certificate in Religious Studies |
| CEO | Chief Education Officer |
| CTC | City Technology College |
| CME | Continuing Ministerial Education |
| CPD | Continuing Professional Development |
| DBE | Diocesan Board of Education |
| DDE | Diocesan Director of Education |
| DfEE | Department for Education and Employment |
| ESTYN | Her Majesty's Inspectorate for Education and Training in Wales |
| F | Foundation School |
| FE | Further Education |
| GCSE | General Certificate of Secondary Education |
| GNVQ | General National Vocational Qualification |
| HEFCE | Higher Education Funding Council for England |
| HESA | Higher Education Statistics Agency |
| ITT | Initial Teacher Training |
| LEA | Local Education Authority |
| LMS | Local Management of Schools |
| NQT | Newly Qualified Teacher |
| OFSTED | Office for Standards in Education |
| PCC | Parochial Church Council |
| PFI | Private Finance Initiative |
| PGCE | Postgraduate Certificate in Education |
| QTS | Qualified Teacher Status |
| RE | Religious Education |
| SACRE | Standing Advisory Committee on Religious Education |
| SATs | Standard Assessment Tests |
| TTA | Teacher Training Agency |
| VA | Voluntary Aided |
| VC | Voluntary Controlled |

# Index

administration 48-9, 61, 82
admissions policies 19, 24, 76, 77–8, 84
    and distinctiveness 27–30, 33
    in ex-Community schools 44
    'open' and 'foundation' places 30, 78
    and pupils of other faiths 29, 80
    and special needs 30
Affiliation Schemes 26, 39
Ainsworth, Janina 57
Archbishops' Council, recommendations to 40, 75
Arnold, Matthew 12
Association of Anglican Secondary School Headteachers 36, 48, 52, 61
Association of Christian Teachers 52

'Beacon' schools 38
Bradford diocese 36
British Humanist Association 1, 16–17
buildings 25, 83

capital costs 26, 37, 40–2, 83
Chair of governing body 44, 45, 55, 61, 62, 75, 77, 84
chaplaincy 19, 31, 55, 56, 58, 66, 67, 71, 92
Chief Education Officers 27
child protection policies 79
choice, parental xi, 16, 17–18, 28
Church Colleges' Certificates 51, 67, 69, 70, 73
    and distance learning 48, 52, 62, 80
    for governors 61–2
Church of England Board of Education ix, 41, 48, 57, 61, 63, 64, 78, 82
Church schools
    categories *see* Foundation Schools; Voluntary Aided schools; Voluntary Controlled schools
    Church's purposes in 12–15, 18, 30
    effectiveness of 10–11, 21
    as family learning centres 10
    increased provision of 34–44
    justification for 11, 19
    *see also* parishes, and school; primary schools; secondary schools
citizenship, and religious education 23
City Academies 39, 40, 41, 42
clergy 9, 47, 52, 53–4, 75
    as Chair of governing body 55, 61, 75, 84
    and Community schools 53, 59, 75
    training xii, 9, 53, 57–9, 72, 75, 81
Code of Practice on School Admissions 27, 30, 77
colleges of higher education 65–72, 80–1, 89–90
    and award of degrees 66, 68, 80
    and chaplaincy 66, 67, 71, 92
    and clergy training 58, 59, 72, 75, 81
    distinctiveness xii, 1, 4, 21, 66–7, 68–71, 73–4, 81
    governance 66
    and leadership development 48, 69, 70
    long-term viability 71–2, 81, 82
    and teachers 50, 52, 65–6, 68–70, 73, 91–2
    and Visitations 70, 72
community
    and admissions policies 27, 30, 78, 80
    relationships with 15–16, 19–20, 23, 24, 36, 39, 48–9
Community schools
    Christian teachers in 4, 9, 50, 52, 73, 77, 92
    distinctiveness of 17

    partnership with 13, 19, 23, 39–40
    and religious education 23
    as Voluntary schools 37–8, 40–2, 43–4, 76
    *see also* Affiliation Schemes; clergy
Council of Church Colleges 65, 72
curriculum 20, 21–2, 67, 69

deaneries, role of 9, 54, 55, 79
deputy heads xi, 4, 18
development gains 40, 42
diocesan boards of education 23, 32, 53, 58, 62–4
    and accountability 63–4, 78
    and LEAs 25, 63
    and resources 26, 41–2, 63, 78
dioceses
    and admissions policies 28, 30, 77–8
    and capital costs 26, 40–1
    and Church colleges 67, 72, 80
    and clergy training 59
    and Community schools 23
directors of education 25–6, 63, 64
    and ecumenical approaches 31, 76
    and governor training 61–2
    and independent schools 32, 78
    and LEAs xi, 24–6, 63, 76
    and parishes 55, 75–6
    and religious education 22, 23
    and school provision 34–40, 41, 76–7, 85–6
    and support for teachers and heads 47, 50, 52, 61, 77
    and Voluntary Controlled schools 23, 24
distinctiveness xi, 2, 3–4, 10, 19–33
    in admissions policies 27–30, 33
    in curriculum 20, 21–2
    and ecumenism 30–1
    and governing body 19, 79
    and inclusiveness 16–17, 27, 29, 48, 67
    of independent schools 32
    in leadership 60
    and LEAs 24–7
    in religious education 20, 22–3
    and status of school 19, 20, 23–4, 28, 76, 78, 80
    and teachers 47
    *see also* Church colleges
Durham Commission of Enquiry 12–13

ecumenism 30–1, 40, 43–4, 64, 76
Education Acts
    1870 6
    1944 6, 41
    1996 22
Education (Schools) Act 1992 21
Education Sunday 52, 54, 79
ethos 9, 15, 24, 28, 30, 31, 43, 83
    statement of 14, 20, 22, 79
Eucharist, in schools 21, 56–7
experience, of Christian faith 10–11, 12, 14–16, 21, 29

failing schools 43–4, 47
faith, experience of 10–11, 12, 14–16, 21, 29
faiths, non-Christian 12, 15–16, 17, 20–1
    and admissions policies 29, 80
    and religious education 22
    and worship 21
festivals, observance of 19, 20

Foundation schools 7, 19, 76, 83–4
'Fresh Start' schools 29, 43–4
fund raising, national initiative 37, 40–1, 75, 78
*A Future in Partnership* 13

GCSE
   in religious studies 22, 51, 52, 79
   results 18, 87–8
governing bodies
   and administration 61
   and admissions policies 27–30, 80, 84
   and capital costs 37, 40–1, 42, 83
   Chair 44, 45, 55, 61, 62, 75, 77, 84
   and distinctiveness 19, 79
   and ethos statement 20, 79, 83
   and headteachers 45, 77, 83
   in independent schools 32
   and LEA services 25
   and parents 46, 52, 79, 84
   and religious education 20, 22
   and support for staff 45–7, 52, 77, 79
   and training 25, 61–2, 69, 73
   in Voluntary Aided schools 7, 8, 13, 24, 28–9, 37, 55, 83–4
   in Voluntary Controlled schools 7, 19, 28, 83–4
Green Paper (CM 5050) 1, 8, 37, 38–9, 42–3
growth, spiritual 12, 22, 56–7, 60, 73
Guildford Diocese, and Affiliation schemes 39

headteachers xi, 1, 4, 7, 18, 20, 60–1
   and administration 48–9, 82
   appointment 25, 55
   and clergy 55, 75–6
   and governing body 45, 77, 83
   of new Church schools 38
   and parish 46, 52, 75–6, 77, 78
   and religious education 22
   Service of Commissioning 52, 77
   of small primary schools 49, 79, 82
   and staff 92
   support for 41, 47, 61, 73
Higher Education Funding Council 70, 71, 81, 82

inclusiveness 15–16, 36
   and distinctiveness 16–17, 27, 29, 48, 67
   and worship 16, 56
independent schools, Anglican xii, 32–3, 78
inspection 18, 21, 22, 43, 51, 84

knowledge, of Christian faith 10–11, 12, 14, 21

leadership
   development of xi-xii, 4, 18, 38, 45, 47–9, 69, 70, 77, 82
   *see also* deputy heads; headteachers
Learning and Skills Councils 7, 39
local education authorities 1, 4, 7, 13, 19, 33, 34
   and admissions policies 27–8, 84
   and Community schools 43–4
   and dioceses xi, 24–6, 63, 76
   and governor services 25
   and provision of new schools xi, 36–7, 40–1, 42, 43–4
   and status of new schools 24, 76

mentoring 61, 76
Methodist Church 6
mission
   and admissions policies 29
   and Church colleges 68
   and clergy training 59
   and increased school provision 1, 34, 37, 39–40
   and independent schools 31
   and proselytism 12, 15, 24, 43
   and role of Church schools ix, xi, 1–5, 9–10, 11, 13–14, 54, 75
   and role of parishes 47, 79

National College for School Leadership 48, 82

national fund, proposed xi, 37, 40–1, 75, 78
National Professional Qualification for Headship 48
National Secular Society 1, 16
National Society ix, 6, 22, 32, 41, 52, 55, 57, 64, 78, 82
needs
   social/economic xii, 18, 24, 27, 29, 30, 39–40, 49, 76
   special educational 27, 30, 40, 76, 77
nurture, and role of Church school 11, 12–15, 27, 29–30, 47, 60, 80

OFSTED inspections 26, 43, 51, 84, 88

parents
   and choice of schools xi, 16, 17–18, 28
   and Community schools 43
   and desire for Christian education 12, 13–14, 28, 34, 37
   and governing bodies 46, 52, 79, 84
   involvement in education 11, 80
   of other world faiths 15, 16, 17
   outreach to 10, 11
parishes
   and prayer for schools 20, 79
   and school xi, xii, 2–3, 4, 9–10, 11, 19–20, 23, 53–6, 75–6, 78–9
   and teachers and teaching 45–7, 50, 77
partnership 2–3, 75
   *see also* community; independent schools; local education authorities; parishes, and school; state
PCCs, and Church schools 46, 54, 55, 78
performance, educational 17–18, 22, 60
prayer for schools 20, 79
primary schools
   existing provision of 6, 34–5, 85
   and inclusiveness 16
   proposed increase in xi, 13, 30, 39, 77
   small 48–9, 79, 82
Private Finance Initiative 37, 41
proselytism, and mission 12, 15, 24, 43

recommendations 1, 75–82
   on admissions policies 28, 29, 30, 33, 77–8, 80
   to Church colleges xii, 67, 68, 69–70, 71, 72, 80–1
   on clergy training 59, 75
   to dioceses 63–4, 67, 75–8, 80
   on distinctiveness xi, 20–1, 28, 33
   to governing bodies 61–2, 77, 79–80
   on headteachers 48–9, 61, 75–6, 78, 79
   on independent schools xii, 32
   to parishes and deaneries xi, 54–5, 75–6, 78–9
   on provision of Church schools 35, 37, 39–40, 63, 75, 76–7
   on religious education 22, 76, 79
   on task forces 41
   on teacher training 51
   on teachers 47, 48, 50, 52, 77, 78, 79
   on village schools 20, 80
   on Voluntary Aided schools 23, 24, 30, 33, 76
   on Voluntary Controlled schools 23, 28, 76
religious education 9, 51, 52, 76, 79, 82, 84
   Agreed Syllabuses 25
   and distinctiveness 20, 22–3
   training in 22, 26, 67
Roman Catholic Church, and schools xi, 6–7, 50–1, 64
Runcie, Robert 4

School Organization Committee 7, 25, 37, 44
School Standards and Framework Act 1998 7, 34, 41
schools see Church schools; primary schools; secondary schools
*Schools Building on Success* (Green Paper CM 5050) 1, 8, 36, 38–9, 42–3
Schools Inspections Act 1996 21
secondary schools
   admissions policies 29
   chaplaincy in 19, 56
   demand for places xi, 10, 36, 37

existing provision 2, 10, 34–7, 86
increased provision xi, xii, 1, 4, 6, 8, 13, 18, 30, 36–42, 64, 75
independent 31
and local parishes 54
and religious education 22–3, 52, 79
Voluntary Aided 29, 80
Voluntary Controlled 28
see also GCSE
selection 24, 27
service, as Church's purpose in education 11, 12–15, 19, 23, 27, 30
signs, and identity 20, 32
Slade, Ray 38
Special schools, Christian teachers in 50, 52, 77
Sponsors, Voluntary Sector 7, 39, 42
standards, academic 17–18, 22, 47, 60, 87–8
Standards Fund 43
Standing Advisory Committees for Religious Education 23, 25
state
partnerships with xi, 1, 4, 6–7, 13, 33, 34, 42–3, 61, 63, 82
and provision of education 3, 6, 19
symbols, Christian 20

task forces, regional 41, 64, 78
teacher training 22, 51–2, 65–6, 68–70, 80–81, 82, 91–2
Initial Teacher Training 65–6, 69
for management 48
and religious education 22, 26, 73
Teacher Training Agency 22, 70, 71, 81, 82
teachers 45–53
and administration 48, 61
and Christian commitment 7, 24, 83
and Continuing Professional Development 69, 70, 73–4, 77, 79, 80, 92
as future leaders 47–8, 77
male 48, 78

from minority ethnic groups 48, 78
morale of 45–7, 49, 52, 77, 79
recruitment and retention xi-xii, 1, 4, 45, 48, 50–1
of religious education 22, 23, 73, 82, 84
theological colleges 53, 57–9, 81
Transfer of Undertakings (Protection of Employment) 44

Value Added Tax 40
villages, and Church schools 19, 20, 23, 27, 48–9, 80
vocation 91–2
teaching as xii, 1, 4, 50, 51, 52, 72, 73–4, 77, 80, 82
Voluntary Aided schools 6–8, 13, 23, 33, 34, 76, 83–4
admissions policies 19, 24, 28–30, 77–8, 80, 84
capital costs 26, 37, 40–1, 42, 83
and Community schools 38
governing body 7, 8, 13, 24, 28–9, 55, 83–4
and LEAs 26
as neighbourhood schools 28, 76
and religious education 22, 84
structural benefits of 24
Voluntary Controlled schools 6–7, 23, 34, 76, 83–4
admissions policies 19, 27–8, 76, 80, 84
and capital costs 37, 41, 42, 83
and change of status 24, 28
and distinctiveness 19, 20, 28, 76, 80
in villages 19, 20, 23, 27, 49–50, 80

Woodard Corporation 31
worship 9, 15, 20, 23, 26, 55, 56–7, 83
in Church colleges 67, 72, 73
inclusive 16, 56
and other world faiths 21
in parish church 19–20, 56, 83
quality of 22

young people
mission to xi, 3, 12, 14
and worship 9–11, 34, 5

99

www.ingramcontent.com/pod-product-compliance
Lightning Source LLC
Chambersburg PA
CBHW081420300426
44110CB00016BA/2332